Workflow and Collaboration
Complete Self-Assessment Guide

The guidance in this Self-Assessment is based on Workflow and Collaboration best practices and standards in business process architecture, design and quality management. The guidance is also based on the professional judgment of the individual collaborators listed in the Acknowledgments.

Notice of rights

Trademarks

Table of Contents

About The Art of Service   8
Acknowledgments   9
Included Resources - how to access   9

Your feedback is invaluable to us   11
Purpose of this Self-Assessment   11
How to use the Self-Assessment   12
Workflow and Collaboration
Scorecard Example   14

Workflow and Collaboration
Scorecard   15

BEGINNING OF THE
SELF-ASSESSMENT: 16
CRITERION #1: RECOGNIZE   17

CRITERION #2: DEFINE: 24

CRITERION #3: MEASURE: 35

CRITERION #4: ANALYZE: 48

CRITERION #5: IMPROVE: 57

CRITERION #6: CONTROL: 69

CRITERION #7: SUSTAIN: 80
Workflow and Collaboration and Managing Projects, Criteria
for Project Managers: 105
1.0 Initiating Process Group: Workflow and Collaboration 106

1.1 Project Charter: Workflow and Collaboration   108

1.2 Stakeholder Register: Workflow and Collaboration   110

1.3 Stakeholder Analysis Matrix: Workflow and Collaboration
111

2.0 Planning Process Group: Workflow and Collaboration 113

2.1 Project Management Plan: Workflow and Collaboration
115

2.2 Scope Management Plan: Workflow and Collaboration
117

2.3 Requirements Management Plan: Workflow and
Collaboration   119

2.4 Requirements Documentation: Workflow and
Collaboration   121

2.5 Requirements Traceability Matrix: Workflow and
Collaboration   123

2.6 Project Scope Statement: Workflow and Collaboration
125

2.7 Assumption and Constraint Log: Workflow and
Collaboration   127

2.8 Work Breakdown Structure: Workflow and Collaboration
129

2.9 WBS Dictionary: Workflow and Collaboration   131

2.10 Schedule Management Plan: Workflow and
Collaboration   134

2.11 Activity List: Workflow and Collaboration   136

2.12 Activity Attributes: Workflow and Collaboration   138

2.13 Milestone List: Workflow and Collaboration   140

2.14 Network Diagram: Workflow and Collaboration   142

2.15 Activity Resource Requirements: Workflow and
Collaboration   144

2.16 Resource Breakdown Structure: Workflow and
Collaboration   145

2.17 Activity Duration Estimates: Workflow and
Collaboration   147

2.18 Duration Estimating Worksheet: Workflow and
Collaboration   149

2.19 Project Schedule: Workflow and Collaboration   151

2.20 Cost Management Plan: Workflow and Collaboration
153

2.21 Activity Cost Estimates: Workflow and Collaboration 155

2.22 Cost Estimating Worksheet: Workflow and Collaboration
157

2.23 Cost Baseline: Workflow and Collaboration   159

2.24 Quality Management Plan: Workflow and Collaboration
161

2.25 Quality Metrics: Workflow and Collaboration   163

2.26 Process Improvement Plan: Workflow and Collaboration
165

2.27 Responsibility Assignment Matrix: Workflow and
Collaboration   167

2.28 Roles and Responsibilities: Workflow and Collaboration 169

2.29 Human Resource Management Plan: Workflow and Collaboration 171

2.30 Communications Management Plan: Workflow and Collaboration 173

2.31 Risk Management Plan: Workflow and Collaboration 175

2.32 Risk Register: Workflow and Collaboration 177

2.33 Probability and Impact Assessment: Workflow and Collaboration 179

2.34 Probability and Impact Matrix: Workflow and Collaboration 181

2.35 Risk Data Sheet: Workflow and Collaboration 183

2.36 Procurement Management Plan: Workflow and Collaboration 185

2.37 Source Selection Criteria: Workflow and Collaboration 187

2.38 Stakeholder Management Plan: Workflow and Collaboration 189

2.39 Change Management Plan: Workflow and Collaboration 191

3.0 Executing Process Group: Workflow and Collaboration 193

3.1 Team Member Status Report: Workflow and Collaboration 195

3.2 Change Request: Workflow and Collaboration   197

3.3 Change Log: Workflow and Collaboration   199

3.4 Decision Log: Workflow and Collaboration   201

3.5 Quality Audit: Workflow and Collaboration   203

3.6 Team Directory: Workflow and Collaboration   206

3.7 Team Operating Agreement: Workflow and Collaboration   208

3.8 Team Performance Assessment: Workflow and Collaboration   210

3.9 Team Member Performance Assessment: Workflow and Collaboration   212

3.10 Issue Log: Workflow and Collaboration   214

4.0 Monitoring and Controlling Process Group: Workflow and Collaboration   216

4.1 Project Performance Report: Workflow and Collaboration   218

4.2 Variance Analysis: Workflow and Collaboration   220

4.3 Earned Value Status: Workflow and Collaboration   222

4.4 Risk Audit: Workflow and Collaboration   224

4.5 Contractor Status Report: Workflow and Collaboration   226

4.6 Formal Acceptance: Workflow and Collaboration   228

5.0 Closing Process Group: Workflow and Collaboration   230

5.1 Procurement Audit: Workflow and Collaboration   232

5.2 Contract Close-Out: Workflow and Collaboration   234

5.3 Project or Phase Close-Out: Workflow and Collaboration
                                                        236

5.4 Lessons Learned: Workflow and Collaboration   238
Index   241

About The Art of Service

The Art of Service, Business Process Architects since 2000, is dedicated to helping stakeholders achieve excellence.

Defining, designing, creating, and implementing a process to solve a stakeholders challenge or meet an objective is the most valuable role… In EVERY group, company, organization and department.

Unless you're talking a one-time, single-use project, there should be a process. Whether that process is managed and implemented by humans, AI, or a combination of the two, it needs to be designed by someone with a complex enough perspective to ask the right questions.

Someone capable of asking the right questions and step back and say, 'What are we really trying to accomplish here? And is there a different way to look at it?'

With The Art of Service's Standard Requirements Self-Assessments, we empower people who can do just that — whether their title is marketer, entrepreneur, manager, salesperson, consultant, Business Process Manager, executive assistant, IT Manager, CIO etc... —they are the people who rule the future. They are people who watch the process as it happens, and ask the right questions to make the process work better.

Contact us when you need any support with this Self-Assessment and any help with templates, blue-prints and examples of standard documents you might need:

http://theartofservice.com
service@theartofservice.com

Acknowledgments

This checklist was developed under the auspices of The Art of Service, chaired by Gerardus Blokdyk.

Representatives from several client companies participated in the preparation of this Self-Assessment.

Our deepest gratitude goes out to Matt Champagne, Ph.D. Surveys Expert, for his invaluable help and advise in structuring the Self Assessment.

In addition, we are thankful for the design and printing services provided.

Included Resources - how to access

Included with your purchase of the book is the Workflow and Collaboration Self-Assessment Spreadsheet Dashboard which contains all questions and Self-Assessment areas and auto-generates insights, graphs, and project RACI planning - all with examples to get you started right away.

How? Simply send an email to
access@theartofservice.com
with this books' title in the subject to get the Workflow and Collaboration Self Assessment Tool right away.

You will receive the following contents with New and Updated specific criteria:
- The latest quick edition of the book in PDF
- The latest complete edition of the book in PDF, which criteria correspond to the criteria in...
- The Self-Assessment Excel Dashboard, and...
- Example pre-filled Self-Assessment Excel Dashboard to get familiar with results generation
- ...plus an extra, special, resource that helps you with project managing.

INCLUDES LIFETIME SELF ASSESSMENT UPDATES

Every self assessment comes with Lifetime Updates and Lifetime Free Updated Books. Lifetime Updates is an industry-first feature which allows you to receive verified self assessment updates, ensuring you always have the most accurate information at your fingertips.

Get it now- you will be glad you did - do it now, before you forget.

Send an email to **access@theartofservice.com** with this books' title in the subject to get the Workflow and Collaboration Self Assessment Tool right away.

Your feedback is invaluable to us

If you recently bought this book, we would love to hear from you! You can do this by writing a review on amazon (or the online store where you purchased this book) about your last purchase! As part of our continual service improvement process, we love to hear real client experiences and feedback.

How does it work?
To post a review on Amazon, just log in to your account and click on the Create Your Own Review button (under Customer Reviews) of the relevant product page. You can find examples of product reviews in Amazon. If you purchased from another online store, simply follow their procedures.

What happens when I submit my review?
Once you have submitted your review, send us an email at review@theartofservice.com with the link to your review so we can properly thank you for your feedback.

Purpose of this Self-Assessment

This Self-Assessment has been developed to improve understanding of the requirements and elements of Workflow and Collaboration, based on best practices and standards in business process architecture, design and quality management.

It is designed to allow for a rapid Self-Assessment to determine how closely existing management practices and procedures correspond to the elements of the Self-Assessment.

The criteria of requirements and elements of Workflow and Collaboration have been rephrased in the format of a Self-Assessment questionnaire, with a seven-criterion scoring system, as explained in this document.

In this format, even with limited background knowledge of

Workflow and Collaboration, a manager can quickly review existing operations to determine how they measure up to the standards. This in turn can serve as the starting point of a 'gap analysis' to identify management tools or system elements that might usefully be implemented in the organization to help improve overall performance.

How to use the Self-Assessment

On the following pages are a series of questions to identify to what extent your Workflow and Collaboration initiative is complete in comparison to the requirements set in standards.

To facilitate answering the questions, there is a space in front of each question to enter a score on a scale of '1' to '5'.

1 Strongly Disagree

2 Disagree

3 Neutral

4 Agree

5 Strongly Agree

Read the question and rate it with the following in front of mind:

'In my belief,
the answer to this question is clearly defined'.

There are two ways in which you can choose to interpret this statement;
1. how aware are you that the answer to the question is clearly defined
2. for more in-depth analysis you can choose to gather

evidence and confirm the answer to the question. This obviously will take more time, most Self-Assessment users opt for the first way to interpret the question and dig deeper later on based on the outcome of the overall Self-Assessment.

A score of '1' would mean that the answer is not clear at all, where a '5' would mean the answer is crystal clear and defined. Leave emtpy when the question is not applicable or you don't want to answer it, you can skip it without affecting your score. Write your score in the space provided.

After you have responded to all the appropriate statements in each section, compute your average score for that section, using the formula provided, and round to the nearest tenth. Then transfer to the corresponding spoke in the Workflow and Collaboration Scorecard on the second next page of the Self-Assessment.

Your completed Workflow and Collaboration Scorecard will give you a clear presentation of which Workflow and Collaboration areas need attention.

Workflow and Collaboration Scorecard Example

Example of how the finalized Scorecard can look like:

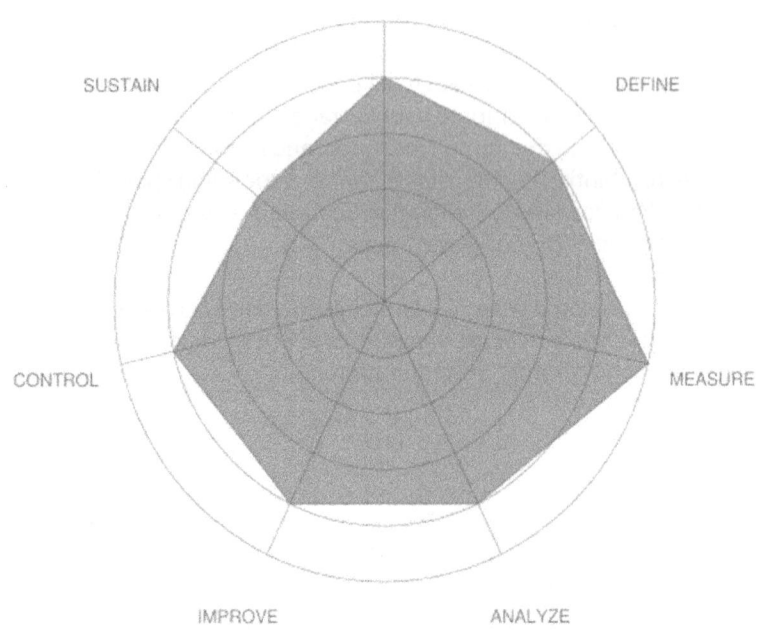

Workflow and Collaboration Scorecard

Your Scores:

BEGINNING OF THE SELF-ASSESSMENT:

CRITERION #1: RECOGNIZE

INTENT: Be aware of the need for change. Recognize that there is an unfavorable variation, problem or symptom.

In my belief, the answer to this question is clearly defined:

5 Strongly Agree

4 Agree

3 Neutral

2 Disagree

1 Strongly Disagree

1. What would happen if Workflow and Collaboration weren't done?
<--- Score

2. How much are sponsors, customers, partners, stakeholders involved in Workflow and Collaboration? In other words, what are the risks, if Workflow and Collaboration does not deliver successfully?
<--- Score

3. What problems are you facing and how do you consider Workflow and Collaboration will circumvent those obstacles?
<--- Score

4. Who needs to know about Workflow and Collaboration ?
<--- Score

5. Are controls defined to recognize and contain problems?
<--- Score

6. Will new equipment/products be required to facilitate Workflow and Collaboration delivery for example is new software needed?
<--- Score

7. Consider your own Workflow and Collaboration project. what types of organizational problems do you think might be causing or affecting your problem, based on the work done so far?
<--- Score

8. What situation(s) led to this Workflow and Collaboration Self Assessment?
<--- Score

9. How do you assess your Workflow and Collaboration workforce capability and capacity needs, including skills, competencies, and staffing levels?
<--- Score

10. Are there Workflow and Collaboration problems

defined?
<--- Score

11. What should be considered when identifying available resources, constraints, and deadlines?
<--- Score

12. What are the expected benefits of Workflow and Collaboration to the business?
<--- Score

13. Who else hopes to benefit from it?
<--- Score

14. What prevents me from making the changes I know will make me a more effective Workflow and Collaboration leader?
<--- Score

15. As a sponsor, customer or management, how important is it to meet goals, objectives?
<--- Score

16. What information do users need?
<--- Score

17. Does Workflow and Collaboration create potential expectations in other areas that need to be recognized and considered?
<--- Score

18. Are there any specific expectations or concerns about the Workflow and Collaboration team, Workflow and Collaboration itself?
<--- Score

19. How does it fit into our organizational needs and tasks?

<--- Score

20. What do we need to start doing?

<--- Score

21. Who had the original idea?

<--- Score

22. Does our organization need more Workflow and Collaboration education?

<--- Score

23. Do we know what we need to know about this topic?

<--- Score

24. Are there recognized Workflow and Collaboration problems?

<--- Score

25. How are the Workflow and Collaboration's objectives aligned to the organization's overall business strategy?

<--- Score

26. How can auditing be a preventative security measure?

<--- Score

27. What is the smallest subset of the problem we can usefully solve?

<--- Score

28. Will Workflow and Collaboration deliverables need

to be tested and, if so, by whom?

<--- Score

29. Will it solve real problems?

<--- Score

30. Is it clear when you think of the day ahead of you what activities and tasks you need to complete?

<--- Score

31. Why do we need to keep records?

<--- Score

32. What vendors make products that address the Workflow and Collaboration needs?

<--- Score

33. For your Workflow and Collaboration project, identify and describe the business environment. is there more than one layer to the business environment?

<--- Score

34. What are the business objectives to be achieved with Workflow and Collaboration?

<--- Score

35. Can Management personnel recognize the monetary benefit of Workflow and Collaboration?

<--- Score

36. How do we Identify specific Workflow and Collaboration investment and emerging trends?

<--- Score

37. What else needs to be measured?
<--- Score

38. Who defines the rules in relation to any given issue?
<--- Score

39. What tools and technologies are needed for a custom Workflow and Collaboration project?
<--- Score

40. How do you identify the kinds of information that you will need?
<--- Score

41. What training and capacity building actions are needed to implement proposed reforms?
<--- Score

42. Think about the people you identified for your Workflow and Collaboration project and the project responsibilities you would assign to them. what kind of training do you think they would need to perform these responsibilities effectively?
<--- Score

43. When a Workflow and Collaboration manager recognizes a problem, what options are available?
<--- Score

44. What does Workflow and Collaboration success mean to the stakeholders?
<--- Score

45. How are you going to measure success?
<--- Score

46. Will a response program recognize when a crisis occurs and provide some level of response?
<--- Score

47. Cloud management for Workflow and Collaboration do we really need one?
<--- Score

Add up total points for this section:
_ _ _ _ _ = Total points for this section

Divided by: _ _ _ _ _ _ (number of statements answered) = _ _ _ _ _ _
Average score for this section

Transfer your score to the Workflow and Collaboration Index at the beginning of the Self-Assessment.

CRITERION #2: DEFINE:

INTENT: Formulate the business problem. Define the problem, needs and objectives.

In my belief, the answer to this question is clearly defined:

5 Strongly Agree

4 Agree

3 Neutral

2 Disagree

1 Strongly Disagree

1. In what way can we redefine the criteria of choice in our category in our favor, as Method introduced style and design to cleaning and Virgin America returned glamor to flying?
<--- Score

2. Is full participation by members in regularly held team meetings guaranteed?
<--- Score

3. Is the team sponsored by a champion or business leader?
<--- Score

4. What are the compelling business reasons for embarking on Workflow and Collaboration?
<--- Score

5. What defines Best in Class?
<--- Score

6. Is Workflow and Collaboration currently on schedule according to the plan?
<--- Score

7. Is the improvement team aware of the different versions of a process: what they think it is vs. what it actually is vs. what it should be vs. what it could be?
<--- Score

8. Are customer(s) identified and segmented according to their different needs and requirements?
<--- Score

9. Have the customer needs been translated into specific, measurable requirements? How?
<--- Score

10. How is the team tracking and documenting its work?
<--- Score

11. What are the boundaries of the scope? What is in bounds and what is not? What is the start point? What is the stop point?

<--- Score

12. What constraints exist that might impact the team?
<--- Score

13. Do we all define Workflow and Collaboration in the same way?
<--- Score

14. Does the team have regular meetings?
<--- Score

15. Is the team adequately staffed with the desired cross-functionality? If not, what additional resources are available to the team?
<--- Score

16. Who defines (or who defined) the rules and roles?
<--- Score

17. Is a fully trained team formed, supported, and committed to work on the Workflow and Collaboration improvements?
<--- Score

18. How often are the team meetings?
<--- Score

19. How will the Workflow and Collaboration team and the organization measure complete success of Workflow and Collaboration?
<--- Score

20. Is there a critical path to deliver Workflow and Collaboration results?

<--- Score

21. Are roles and responsibilities formally defined?
<--- Score

22. Has the direction changed at all during the course of Workflow and Collaboration? If so, when did it change and why?
<--- Score

23. When is the estimated completion date?
<--- Score

24. What critical content must be communicated – who, what, when, where, and how?
<--- Score

25. In what way can we redefine the criteria of choice clients have in our category in our favor?
<--- Score

26. Has everyone on the team, including the team leaders, been properly trained?
<--- Score

27. Has anyone else (internal or external to the organization) attempted to solve this problem or a similar one before? If so, what knowledge can be leveraged from these previous efforts?
<--- Score

28. Are Required Metrics Defined?
<--- Score

29. Are task requirements clearly defined?
<--- Score

30. Has a project plan, Gantt chart, or similar been developed/completed?
<--- Score

31. Will team members regularly document their Workflow and Collaboration work?
<--- Score

32. Have all of the relationships been defined properly?
<--- Score

33. Is data collected and displayed to better understand customer(s) critical needs and requirements.
<--- Score

34. Have all basic functions of Workflow and Collaboration been defined?
<--- Score

35. How does the Workflow and Collaboration manager ensure against scope creep?
<--- Score

36. Has a team charter been developed and communicated?
<--- Score

37. Who are the Workflow and Collaboration improvement team members, including Management Leads and Coaches?
<--- Score

38. Are team charters developed?

<--- Score

39. How would you define the culture here?
<--- Score

40. When was the Workflow and Collaboration start date?
<--- Score

41. Is there a completed, verified, and validated high-level 'as is' (not 'should be' or 'could be') business process map?
<--- Score

42. What customer feedback methods were used to solicit their input?
<--- Score

43. Are customers identified and high impact areas defined?
<--- Score

44. Are improvement team members fully trained on Workflow and Collaboration?
<--- Score

45. Are business processes mapped?
<--- Score

46. Do the problem and goal statements meet the SMART criteria (specific, measurable, attainable, relevant, and time-bound)?
<--- Score

47. Has the Workflow and Collaboration work been fairly and/or equitably divided and delegated among

team members who are qualified and capable to perform the work? Has everyone contributed?
<--- Score

48. How can the value of Workflow and Collaboration be defined?
<--- Score

49. Is there a Workflow and Collaboration management charter, including business case, problem and goal statements, scope, milestones, roles and responsibilities, communication plan?
<--- Score

50. Is the Workflow and Collaboration scope manageable?
<--- Score

51. What are the rough order estimates on cost savings/opportunities that Workflow and Collaboration brings?
<--- Score

52. How did the Workflow and Collaboration manager receive input to the development of a Workflow and Collaboration improvement plan and the estimated completion dates/times of each activity?
<--- Score

53. Has/have the customer(s) been identified?
<--- Score

54. How would one define Workflow and Collaboration leadership?
<--- Score

55. How and when will the baselines be defined?
<--- Score

56. What would be the goal or target for a Workflow and Collaboration's improvement team?
<--- Score

57. Has the improvement team collected the 'voice of the customer' (obtained feedback – qualitative and quantitative)?
<--- Score

58. What are the Roles and Responsibilities for each team member and its leadership? Where is this documented?
<--- Score

59. Is it clearly defined in and to your organization what you do?
<--- Score

60. Is the team formed and are team leaders (Coaches and Management Leads) assigned?
<--- Score

61. Are there different segments of customers?
<--- Score

62. Is the scope of Workflow and Collaboration defined?
<--- Score

63. Is the team equipped with available and reliable resources?
<--- Score

64. What key business process output measure(s) does Workflow and Collaboration leverage and how?
<--- Score

65. How was the 'as is' process map developed, reviewed, verified and validated?
<--- Score

66. If substitutes have been appointed, have they been briefed on the Workflow and Collaboration goals and received regular communications as to the progress to date?
<--- Score

67. What baselines are required to be defined and managed?
<--- Score

68. Are there any constraints known that bear on the ability to perform Workflow and Collaboration work? How is the team addressing them?
<--- Score

69. Has a high-level 'as is' process map been completed, verified and validated?
<--- Score

70. What specifically is the problem? Where does it occur? When does it occur? What is its extent?
<--- Score

71. Is Workflow and Collaboration linked to key business goals and objectives?
<--- Score

72. Have specific policy objectives been defined?

<--- Score

73. Are audit criteria, scope, frequency and methods defined?
<--- Score

74. Is there regularly 100% attendance at the team meetings? If not, have appointed substitutes attended to preserve cross-functionality and full representation?
<--- Score

75. Will team members perform Workflow and Collaboration work when assigned and in a timely fashion?
<--- Score

76. Are different versions of process maps needed to account for the different types of inputs?
<--- Score

77. What are the dynamics of the communication plan?
<--- Score

78. Is the current 'as is' process being followed? If not, what are the discrepancies?
<--- Score

79. Is there a completed SIPOC representation, describing the Suppliers, Inputs, Process, Outputs, and Customers?
<--- Score

80. Are approval levels defined for contracts and supplements to contracts?

<--- Score

81. Is Workflow and Collaboration Required?
<--- Score

82. What is the minimum educational requirement for potential new hires?
<--- Score

83. Are accountability and ownership for Workflow and Collaboration clearly defined?
<--- Score

84. How will variation in the actual durations of each activity be dealt with to ensure that the expected Workflow and Collaboration results are met?
<--- Score

85. When are meeting minutes sent out? Who is on the distribution list?
<--- Score

86. How do you keep key subject matter experts in the loop?
<--- Score

Add up total points for this section:
_____ = Total points for this section

Divided by: _____ (number of statements answered) = _____
Average score for this section

Transfer your score to the Workflow and Collaboration Index at the beginning of the Self-Assessment.

CRITERION #3: MEASURE:

INTENT: Gather the correct data.
Measure the current performance and
evolution of the situation.

In my belief, the answer to this
question is clearly defined:

5 Strongly Agree

4 Agree

3 Neutral

2 Disagree

1 Strongly Disagree

1. What is measured?
<--- Score

2. How is progress measured?
<--- Score

3. Are the units of measure consistent?
<--- Score

4. What are the uncertainties surrounding estimates of impact?

<--- Score

5. How will you measure your Workflow and Collaboration effectiveness?

<--- Score

6. Will Workflow and Collaboration have an impact on current business continuity, disaster recovery processes and/or infrastructure?

<--- Score

7. Does Workflow and Collaboration analysis show the relationships among important Workflow and Collaboration factors?

<--- Score

8. How do you measure success?

<--- Score

9. Why do measure/indicators matter?

<--- Score

10. Is this an issue for analysis or intuition?

<--- Score

11. Meeting the challenge: are missed Workflow and Collaboration opportunities costing us money?

<--- Score

12. How large is the gap between current performance and the customer-specified (goal) performance?

<--- Score

13. Do staff have the necessary skills to collect, analyze, and report data?
<--- Score

14. What about Workflow and Collaboration Analysis of results?
<--- Score

15. How will measures be used to manage and adapt?
<--- Score

16. Does the practice systematically track and analyze outcomes related for accountability and quality improvement?
<--- Score

17. What are the key input variables? What are the key process variables? What are the key output variables?
<--- Score

18. What are my customers expectations and measures?
<--- Score

19. Who should receive measurement reports ?
<--- Score

20. How can we measure the performance?
<--- Score

21. What to measure and why?
<--- Score

22. How do we do risk analysis of rare, cascading, catastrophic events?

<--- Score

23. Was a data collection plan established?
<--- Score

24. Do we aggressively reward and promote the people who have the biggest impact on creating excellent Workflow and Collaboration services/ products?
<--- Score

25. Where is it measured?
<--- Score

26. Are process variation components displayed/ communicated using suitable charts, graphs, plots?
<--- Score

27. What key measures identified indicate the performance of the business process?
<--- Score

28. What are the types and number of measures to use?
<--- Score

29. Is long term and short term variability accounted for?
<--- Score

30. What are your key Workflow and Collaboration organizational performance measures, including key short and longer-term financial measures?
<--- Score

31. Which Stakeholder Characteristics Are Analyzed?

<--- Score

32. Are there any easy-to-implement alternatives to Workflow and Collaboration? Sometimes other solutions are available that do not require the cost implications of a full-blown project?
<--- Score

33. How Will We Measure Success?
<--- Score

34. How to measure lifecycle phases?
<--- Score

35. What are measures?
<--- Score

36. How do your measurements capture actionable Workflow and Collaboration information for use in exceeding your customers expectations and securing your customers engagement?
<--- Score

37. What are the costs of reform?
<--- Score

38. What evidence is there and what is measured?
<--- Score

39. How frequently do we track measures?
<--- Score

40. Are high impact defects defined and identified in the business process?
<--- Score

41. Why should we expend time and effort to implement measurement?
<--- Score

42. Is performance measured?
<--- Score

43. How will success or failure be measured?
<--- Score

44. Among the Workflow and Collaboration product and service cost to be estimated, which is considered hardest to estimate?
<--- Score

45. How do we focus on what is right -not who is right?
<--- Score

46. Why Measure?
<--- Score

47. Is key measure data collection planned and executed, process variation displayed and communicated and performance baselined?
<--- Score

48. Is data collected on key measures that were identified?
<--- Score

49. How can you measure Workflow and Collaboration in a systematic way?
<--- Score

50. Will We Aggregate Measures across Priorities?

<--- Score

51. What should be measured?
<--- Score

52. How will effects be measured?
<--- Score

53. Are you taking your company in the direction of better and revenue or cheaper and cost?
<--- Score

54. Have you found any 'ground fruit' or 'low-hanging fruit' for immediate remedies to the gap in performance?
<--- Score

55. Have the types of risks that may impact Workflow and Collaboration been identified and analyzed?
<--- Score

56. Is a solid data collection plan established that includes measurement systems analysis?
<--- Score

57. What measurements are possible, practicable and meaningful?
<--- Score

58. What is the total cost related to deploying Workflow and Collaboration, including any consulting or professional services?
<--- Score

59. What will be measured?
<--- Score

60. How to measure variability?
<--- Score

61. The approach of traditional Workflow and Collaboration works for detail complexity but is focused on a systematic approach rather than an understanding of the nature of systems themselves. what approach will permit us to deal with the kind of unpredictable emergent behaviors that dynamic complexity can introduce?
<--- Score

62. How are you going to measure success?
<--- Score

63. Are there measurements based on task performance?
<--- Score

64. Have the concerns of stakeholders to help identify and define potential barriers been obtained and analyzed?
<--- Score

65. Is it possible to estimate the impact of unanticipated complexity such as wrong or failed assumptions, feedback, etc. on proposed reforms?
<--- Score

66. Which customers cant participate in our Workflow and Collaboration domain because they lack skills, wealth, or convenient access to existing solutions?
<--- Score

67. What methods are feasible and acceptable to estimate the impact of reforms?
<--- Score

68. Schedule Development, Feasibility Analysis, Workflow and Collaboration Management, Project Closings, Technique: Using the Critical Path Method
<--- Score

69. Have all non-recommended alternatives been analyzed in sufficient detail?
<--- Score

70. What charts has the team used to display the components of variation in the process?
<--- Score

71. What data was collected (past, present, future/ongoing)?
<--- Score

72. Which customers can't participate in our market because they lack skills, wealth, or convenient access to existing solutions?
<--- Score

73. Is data collection planned and executed?
<--- Score

74. Are the measurements objective?
<--- Score

75. What is an unallowable cost?
<--- Score

76. What Relevant Entities could be measured?

<--- Score

77. Is the solution cost-effective?
<--- Score

78. How frequently do you track Workflow and Collaboration measures?
<--- Score

79. Why identify and analyze stakeholders and their interests?
<--- Score

80. When is Knowledge Management Measured?
<--- Score

81. Are we taking our company in the direction of better and revenue or cheaper and cost?
<--- Score

82. What measurements are being captured?
<--- Score

83. How do you identify and analyze stakeholders and their interests?
<--- Score

84. How is the value delivered by Workflow and Collaboration being measured?
<--- Score

85. Can we do Workflow and Collaboration without complex (expensive) analysis?
<--- Score

86. Can We Measure the Return on Analysis?

<--- Score

87. What potential environmental factors impact the Workflow and Collaboration effort?
<--- Score

88. Is there a Performance Baseline?
<--- Score

89. How is Knowledge Management Measured?
<--- Score

90. How are measurements made?
<--- Score

91. How will your organization measure success?
<--- Score

92. What is the right balance of time and resources between investigation, analysis, and discussion and dissemination?
<--- Score

93. Customer Measures: How Do Customers See Us?
<--- Score

94. What are the agreed upon definitions of the high impact areas, defect(s), unit(s), and opportunities that will figure into the process capability metrics?
<--- Score

95. Have changes been properly/adequately analyzed for effect?
<--- Score

96. What has the team done to assure the stability and

accuracy of the measurement process?
<--- Score

97. Are key measures identified and agreed upon?
<--- Score

98. Who participated in the data collection for measurements?
<--- Score

99. Does Workflow and Collaboration systematically track and analyze outcomes for accountability and quality improvement?
<--- Score

100. What are our key indicators that you will measure, analyze and track?
<--- Score

101. Does Workflow and Collaboration analysis isolate the fundamental causes of problems?
<--- Score

102. Does the Workflow and Collaboration task fit the client's priorities?
<--- Score

103. Do we effectively measure and reward individual and team performance?
<--- Score

104. Is Process Variation Displayed/Communicated?
<--- Score

105. What particular quality tools did the team find helpful in establishing measurements?

<--- Score

106. Are losses documented, analyzed, and remedial processes developed to prevent future losses?
<--- Score

107. Why do the measurements/indicators matter?
<--- Score

Add up total points for this section:
_____ = Total points for this section

Divided by: _____ (number of statements answered) = _____
Average score for this section

Transfer your score to the Workflow and Collaboration Index at the beginning of the Self-Assessment.

CRITERION #4: ANALYZE:

INTENT: Analyze causes, assumptions and hypotheses.

In my belief, the answer to this question is clearly defined:

5 Strongly Agree

4 Agree

3 Neutral

2 Disagree

1 Strongly Disagree

1. What process should we select for improvement?
<--- Score

2. What other organizational variables, such as reward systems or communication systems, affect the performance of this Workflow and Collaboration process?
<--- Score

3. What is the cost of poor quality as supported by the

team's analysis?
<--- Score

4. What are your current levels and trends in key Workflow and Collaboration measures or indicators of product and process performance that are important to and directly serve your customers?
<--- Score

5. How do you use Workflow and Collaboration data and information to support organizational decision making and innovation?
<--- Score

6. How do you measure the Operational performance of your key work systems and processes, including productivity, cycle time, and other appropriate measures of process effectiveness, efficiency, and innovation?
<--- Score

7. What are the disruptive Workflow and Collaboration technologies that enable our organization to radically change our business processes?
<--- Score

8. Is the suppliers process defined and controlled?
<--- Score

9. An organizationally feasible system request is one that considers the mission, goals and objectives of the organization. key questions are: is the solution request practical and will it solve a problem or take advantage of an opportunity to

achieve company goals?
<--- Score

10. Record-keeping requirements flow from the records needed as inputs, outputs, controls and for transformation of a Workflow and Collaboration process. ask yourself: are the records needed as inputs to the Workflow and Collaboration process available?
<--- Score

11. Where is the data coming from to measure compliance?
<--- Score

12. Have any additional benefits been identified that will result from closing all or most of the gaps?
<--- Score

13. Is the Workflow and Collaboration process severely broken such that a re-design is necessary?
<--- Score

14. When conducting a business process reengineering study, what should we look for when trying to identify business processes to change?
<--- Score

15. How do we promote understanding that opportunity for improvement is not criticism of the status quo, or the people who created the status quo?
<--- Score

16. Were any designed experiments used to generate

additional insight into the data analysis?
<--- Score

17. Can we add value to the current Workflow and Collaboration decision-making process (largely qualitative) by incorporating uncertainty modeling (more quantitative)?
<--- Score

18. What does the data say about the performance of the business process?
<--- Score

19. What tools were used to narrow the list of possible causes?
<--- Score

20. Think about the functions involved in your Workflow and Collaboration project. what processes flow from these functions?
<--- Score

21. What did the team gain from developing a sub-process map?
<--- Score

22. What quality tools were used to get through the analyze phase?
<--- Score

23. A compounding model resolution with available relevant data can often provide insight towards a solution methodology; which Workflow and Collaboration models, tools and techniques are necessary?
<--- Score

24. Is the gap/opportunity displayed and communicated in financial terms?
<--- Score

25. What conclusions were drawn from the team's data collection and analysis? How did the team reach these conclusions?
<--- Score

26. Do our leaders quickly bounce back from setbacks?
<--- Score

27. Have the problem and goal statements been updated to reflect the additional knowledge gained from the analyze phase?
<--- Score

28. How is the way you as the leader think and process information affecting your organizational culture?
<--- Score

29. Teaches and consults on quality process improvement, project management, and accelerated Workflow and Collaboration techniques
<--- Score

30. Did any value-added analysis or 'lean thinking' take place to identify some of the gaps shown on the 'as is' process map?
<--- Score

31. What tools were used to generate the list of possible causes?
<--- Score

32. Think about some of the processes you undertake within your organization. which do you own?
<--- Score

33. Is the performance gap determined?
<--- Score

34. What were the financial benefits resulting from any 'ground fruit or low-hanging fruit' (quick fixes)?
<--- Score

35. How was the detailed process map generated, verified, and validated?
<--- Score

36. Were there any improvement opportunities identified from the process analysis?
<--- Score

37. Was a cause-and-effect diagram used to explore the different types of causes (or sources of variation)?
<--- Score

38. What successful thing are we doing today that may be blinding us to new growth opportunities?
<--- Score

39. How do mission and objectives affect the Workflow and Collaboration processes of our organization?
<--- Score

40. What other jobs or tasks affect the performance of the steps in the Workflow and

Collaboration process?

<--- Score

41. What are your current levels and trends in key measures or indicators of Workflow and Collaboration product and process performance that are important to and directly serve your customers? how do these results compare with the performance of your competitors and other organizations with similar offerings?

<--- Score

42. How often will data be collected for measures?

<--- Score

43. What controls do we have in place to protect data?

<--- Score

44. What are the revised rough estimates of the financial savings/opportunity for Workflow and Collaboration improvements?

<--- Score

45. What are the best opportunities for value improvement?

<--- Score

46. Are gaps between current performance and the goal performance identified?

<--- Score

47. Do your employees have the opportunity to do what they do best everyday?

<--- Score

48. Identify an operational issue in your

organization. for example, could a particular task be done more quickly or more efficiently?
<--- Score

49. Were Pareto charts (or similar) used to portray the 'heavy hitters' (or key sources of variation)?
<--- Score

50. What were the crucial 'moments of truth' on the process map?
<--- Score

51. How does the organization define, manage, and improve its Workflow and Collaboration processes?
<--- Score

52. Is Data and process analysis, root cause analysis and quantifying the gap/opportunity in place?
<--- Score

53. Was a detailed process map created to amplify critical steps of the 'as is' business process?
<--- Score

54. Do you, as a leader, bounce back quickly from setbacks?
<--- Score

55. What are our Workflow and Collaboration Processes?
<--- Score

56. Did any additional data need to be collected?
<--- Score

Add up total points for this section:

_____ = Total points for this section

Divided by: _____ (number of
statements answered) = _____
Average score for this section

Transfer your score to the Workflow and
Collaboration Index at the beginning of
the Self-Assessment.

CRITERION #5: IMPROVE:

INTENT: Develop a practical solution. Innovate, establish and test the solution and to measure the results.

In my belief, the answer to this question is clearly defined:

5 Strongly Agree

4 Agree

3 Neutral

2 Disagree

1 Strongly Disagree

1. How do we Improve Workflow and Collaboration service perception, and satisfaction?
<--- Score

2. Are new and improved process ('should be') maps developed?
<--- Score

3. Is a contingency plan established?

<--- Score

4. Why improve in the first place?
<--- Score

5. How will you measure the results?
<--- Score

6. Who will be responsible for making the decisions to include or exclude requested changes once Workflow and Collaboration is underway?
<--- Score

7. How to Improve?
<--- Score

8. How will the organization know that the solution worked?
<--- Score

9. What is Workflow and Collaboration's impact on utilizing the best solution(s)?
<--- Score

10. What does the 'should be' process map/design look like?
<--- Score

11. Risk factors: what are the characteristics of Workflow and Collaboration that make it risky?
<--- Score

12. How important is the completion of a recognized college or graduate-level degree program in the hiring decision?
<--- Score

13. How can we improve Workflow and Collaboration?
<--- Score

14. If you could go back in time five years, what decision would you make differently? What is your best guess as to what decision you're making today you might regret five years from now?
<--- Score

15. What needs improvement?
<--- Score

16. Do we combine technical expertise with business knowledge and Workflow and Collaboration Key topics include lifecycles, development approaches, requirements and how to make a business case?
<--- Score

17. What actually has to improve and by how much?
<--- Score

18. How do we measure improved Workflow and Collaboration service perception, and satisfaction?
<--- Score

19. How does the team improve its work?
<--- Score

20. Do we cover the five essential competencies- Communication, Collaboration,Innovation, Adaptability, and Leadership that improve an organization's ability to leverage the new Workflow and Collaboration in a volatile global economy?
<--- Score

21. To what extent does management recognize Workflow and Collaboration as a tool to increase the results?
<--- Score

22. What were the underlying assumptions on the cost-benefit analysis?
<--- Score

23. How significant is the improvement in the eyes of the end user?
<--- Score

24. How do you improve your likelihood of success ?
<--- Score

25. How do you manage and improve your Workflow and Collaboration work systems to deliver customer value and achieve organizational success and sustainability?
<--- Score

26. What is the magnitude of the improvements?
<--- Score

27. What is the team's contingency plan for potential problems occurring in implementation?
<--- Score

28. How can we improve performance?
<--- Score

29. Is there a cost/benefit analysis of optimal solution(s)?
<--- Score

30. Risk events: what are the things that could go wrong?

<--- Score

31. Is the implementation plan designed?

<--- Score

32. How do the Workflow and Collaboration results compare with the performance of your competitors and other organizations with similar offerings?

<--- Score

33. Does the goal represent a desired result that can be measured?

<--- Score

34. How will you know that you have improved?

<--- Score

35. What tools were used to evaluate the potential solutions?

<--- Score

36. What actually has to improve and by how much?

<--- Score

37. What went well, what should change, what can improve?

<--- Score

38. How do we keep improving Workflow and Collaboration?

<--- Score

39. What is the implementation plan?
<--- Score

40. What error proofing will be done to address some of the discrepancies observed in the 'as is' process?
<--- Score

41. How will we know that a change is improvement?
<--- Score

42. Are we using Workflow and Collaboration to communicate information about our Cybersecurity Risk Management programs including the effectiveness of those programs to stakeholders, including boards, investors, auditors, and insurers?
<--- Score

43. For decision problems, how do you develop a decision statement?
<--- Score

44. Is Supporting Workflow and Collaboration documentation required?
<--- Score

45. In the past few months, what is the smallest change we have made that has had the biggest positive result? What was it about that small change that produced the large return?
<--- Score

46. How will the team or the process owner(s) monitor the implementation plan to see that it is working as intended?
<--- Score

47. Was a pilot designed for the proposed solution(s)?
<--- Score

48. What tools were most useful during the improve phase?
<--- Score

49. Describe the design of the pilot and what tests were conducted, if any?
<--- Score

50. Are we Assessing Workflow and Collaboration and Risk?
<--- Score

51. Are there any constraints (technical, political, cultural, or otherwise) that would inhibit certain solutions?
<--- Score

52. What is the Workflow and Collaboration sustainability risk?
<--- Score

53. How do we measure risk?
<--- Score

54. How can skill-level changes improve Workflow and Collaboration?
<--- Score

55. What can we do to improve?
<--- Score

56. What tools were used to tap into the creativity and

encourage 'outside the box' thinking?
<--- Score

57. Is the optimal solution selected based on testing and analysis?
<--- Score

58. How will you know when its improved?
<--- Score

59. Is the measure understandable to a variety of people?
<--- Score

60. Is a solution implementation plan established, including schedule/work breakdown structure, resources, risk management plan, cost/budget, and control plan?
<--- Score

61. How do you measure progress and evaluate training effectiveness?
<--- Score

62. How do we improve productivity?
<--- Score

63. Is the solution technically practical?
<--- Score

64. Who controls the risk?
<--- Score

65. What should a proof of concept or pilot accomplish?
<--- Score

66. Who will be responsible for documenting the Workflow and Collaboration requirements in detail?
<--- Score

67. What is the risk?
<--- Score

68. What are the implications of this decision 10 minutes, 10 months, and 10 years from now?
<--- Score

69. What to do with the results or outcomes of measurements?
<--- Score

70. Who are the people involved in developing and implementing Workflow and Collaboration?
<--- Score

71. What do we want to improve?
<--- Score

72. Is pilot data collected and analyzed?
<--- Score

73. What evaluation strategy is needed and what needs to be done to assure its implementation and use?
<--- Score

74. How do we decide how much to remunerate an employee?
<--- Score

75. Are possible solutions generated and tested?

<--- Score

76. What tools do you use once you have decided on a Workflow and Collaboration strategy and more importantly how do you choose?
<--- Score

77. What communications are necessary to support the implementation of the solution?
<--- Score

78. Who controls key decisions that will be made?
<--- Score

79. What attendant changes will need to be made to ensure that the solution is successful?
<--- Score

80. At what point will vulnerability assessments be performed once Workflow and Collaboration is put into production (e.g., ongoing Risk Management after implementation)?
<--- Score

81. How does the solution remove the key sources of issues discovered in the analyze phase?
<--- Score

82. Were any criteria developed to assist the team in testing and evaluating potential solutions?
<--- Score

83. Explorations of the frontiers of Workflow and Collaboration will help you build influence, improve Workflow and Collaboration, optimize decision making, and sustain change

<--- Score

84. How do we go about Comparing Workflow and Collaboration approaches/solutions?
<--- Score

85. Is there a high likelihood that any recommendations will achieve their intended results?
<--- Score

86. What lessons, if any, from a pilot were incorporated into the design of the full-scale solution?
<--- Score

87. What improvements have been achieved?
<--- Score

88. Who will be using the results of the measurement activities?
<--- Score

89. Can the solution be designed and implemented within an acceptable time period?
<--- Score

90. Are improved process ('should be') maps modified based on pilot data and analysis?
<--- Score

91. How Do We Link Measurement and Risk?
<--- Score

92. Are the best solutions selected?
<--- Score

93. For estimation problems, how do you develop an estimation statement?

<--- Score

94. Is there a small-scale pilot for proposed improvement(s)? What conclusions were drawn from the outcomes of a pilot?

<--- Score

95. What resources are required for the improvement effort?

<--- Score

96. How did the team generate the list of possible solutions?

<--- Score

Add up total points for this section:

_ _ _ _ _ = Total points for this section

Divided by: _ _ _ _ _ _ (number of statements answered) = _ _ _ _ _ _

Average score for this section

Transfer your score to the Workflow and Collaboration Index at the beginning of the Self-Assessment.

CRITERION #6: CONTROL:

INTENT: Implement the practical solution. Maintain the performance and correct possible complications.

In my belief, the answer to this question is clearly defined:

5 Strongly Agree

4 Agree

3 Neutral

2 Disagree

1 Strongly Disagree

1. Does the Workflow and Collaboration performance meet the customer's requirements?
<--- Score

2. What is the recommended frequency of auditing?
<--- Score

3. Who is the Workflow and Collaboration process owner?

<--- Score

4. How will the day-to-day responsibilities for monitoring and continual improvement be transferred from the improvement team to the process owner?
<--- Score

5. What other systems, operations, processes, and infrastructures (hiring practices, staffing, training, incentives/rewards, metrics/dashboards/scorecards, etc.) need updates, additions, changes, or deletions in order to facilitate knowledge transfer and improvements?
<--- Score

6. Is a response plan established and deployed?
<--- Score

7. What is the control/monitoring plan?
<--- Score

8. What are we attempting to measure/monitor?
<--- Score

9. What are the critical parameters to watch?
<--- Score

10. Is there documentation that will support the successful operation of the improvement?
<--- Score

11. Will any special training be provided for results interpretation?
<--- Score

12. Is there a documented and implemented monitoring plan?

<--- Score

13. Are suggested corrective/restorative actions indicated on the response plan for known causes to problems that might surface?

<--- Score

14. Do we monitor the Workflow and Collaboration decisions made and fine tune them as they evolve?

<--- Score

15. What should we measure to verify efficiency gains?

<--- Score

16. How likely is the current Workflow and Collaboration plan to come in on schedule or on budget?

<--- Score

17. Can Workflow and Collaboration be learned?

<--- Score

18. Are pertinent alerts monitored, analyzed and distributed to appropriate personnel?

<--- Score

19. Strategic planning -Workflow and Collaboration relations

<--- Score

20. Do the Workflow and Collaboration decisions we make today help people and the planet tomorrow?

<--- Score

21. Who has control over resources?
<--- Score

22. Is knowledge gained on process shared and institutionalized?
<--- Score

23. What is your theory of human motivation, and how does your compensation plan fit with that view?
<--- Score

24. Were the planned controls working?
<--- Score

25. Is there a transfer of ownership and knowledge to process owner and process team tasked with the responsibilities.
<--- Score

26. What should the next improvement project be that is related to Workflow and Collaboration?
<--- Score

27. In the case of a Workflow and Collaboration project, the criteria for the audit derive from implementation objectives. an audit of a Workflow and Collaboration project involves assessing whether the recommendations outlined for implementation have been met. Can we track that any Workflow and Collaboration project is implemented as planned, and is it working?
<--- Score

28. Is reporting being used or needed?

<--- Score

29. Have new or revised work instructions resulted?
<--- Score

30. Who controls critical resources?
<--- Score

31. Does the response plan contain a definite closed loop continual improvement scheme (e.g., plan-do-check-act)?
<--- Score

32. Does a troubleshooting guide exist or is it needed?
<--- Score

33. Is a response plan in place for when the input, process, or output measures indicate an 'out-of-control' condition?
<--- Score

34. Workflow and Collaboration in management -Strategic planning
<--- Score

35. Will existing staff require re-training, for example, to learn new business processes?
<--- Score

36. Is there a control plan in place for sustaining improvements (short and long-term)?
<--- Score

37. What are the known security controls?
<--- Score

38. How do you select, collect, align, and integrate Workflow and Collaboration data and information for tracking daily operations and overall organizational performance, including progress relative to strategic objectives and action plans?
<--- Score

39. Has the improved process and its steps been standardized?
<--- Score

40. Do you monitor the effectiveness of your Workflow and Collaboration activities?
<--- Score

41. Is there a recommended audit plan for routine surveillance inspections of Workflow and Collaboration's gains?
<--- Score

42. Whats the best design framework for Workflow and Collaboration organization now that, in a post industrial-age if the top-down, command and control model is no longer relevant?
<--- Score

43. What should we measure to verify effectiveness gains?
<--- Score

44. What are the key elements of your Workflow and Collaboration performance improvement system, including your evaluation, organizational learning, and innovation processes?
<--- Score

45. What do we stand for--and what are we against?

<--- Score

46. Does Workflow and Collaboration appropriately measure and monitor risk?

<--- Score

47. Are there documented procedures?

<--- Score

48. How do you encourage people to take control and responsibility?

<--- Score

49. How will new or emerging customer needs/requirements be checked/communicated to orient the process toward meeting the new specifications and continually reducing variation?

<--- Score

50. How can we best use all of our knowledge repositories to enhance learning and sharing?

<--- Score

51. Is new knowledge gained imbedded in the response plan?

<--- Score

52. Are operating procedures consistent?

<--- Score

53. What quality tools were useful in the control phase?

<--- Score

54. How will input, process, and output variables be checked to detect for sub-optimal conditions?
<--- Score

55. Is there a standardized process?
<--- Score

56. How will the process owner verify improvement in present and future sigma levels, process capabilities?
<--- Score

57. Are documented procedures clear and easy to follow for the operators?
<--- Score

58. What is our theory of human motivation, and how does our compensation plan fit with that view?
<--- Score

59. Why is change control necessary?
<--- Score

60. Is there a Workflow and Collaboration Communication plan covering who needs to get what information when?
<--- Score

61. What key inputs and outputs are being measured on an ongoing basis?
<--- Score

62. Where do ideas that reach policy makers and planners as proposals for Workflow and Collaboration strengthening and reform actually originate?

<--- Score

63. Who will be in control?
<--- Score

64. What are your results for key measures or indicators of the accomplishment of your Workflow and Collaboration strategy and action plans, including building and strengthening core competencies?
<--- Score

65. How do our controls stack up?
<--- Score

66. Were the planned controls in place?
<--- Score

67. Against what alternative is success being measured?
<--- Score

68. Implementation Planning- is a pilot needed to test the changes before a full roll out occurs?
<--- Score

69. How will report readings be checked to effectively monitor performance?
<--- Score

70. How might the organization capture best practices and lessons learned so as to leverage improvements across the business?
<--- Score

71. Does job training on the documented procedures

need to be part of the process team's education and training?
<--- Score

72. How do controls support value?
<--- Score

73. Do the decisions we make today help people and the planet tomorrow?
<--- Score

74. Are controls in place and consistently applied?
<--- Score

75. What can you control?
<--- Score

76. Measure, Monitor and Predict Workflow and Collaboration Activities to Optimize Operations and Profitably, and Enhance Outcomes
<--- Score

77. How will the process owner and team be able to hold the gains?
<--- Score

78. What other areas of the organization might benefit from the Workflow and Collaboration team's improvements, knowledge, and learning?
<--- Score

79. Are new process steps, standards, and documentation ingrained into normal operations?
<--- Score

Add up total points for this section:

_____ = Total points for this section

Divided by: _____ (number of statements answered) = _____ Average score for this section

Transfer your score to the Workflow and Collaboration Index at the beginning of the Self-Assessment.

CRITERION #7: SUSTAIN:

INTENT: Retain the benefits.

In my belief, the answer to this question is clearly defined:

5 Strongly Agree

4 Agree

3 Neutral

2 Disagree

1 Strongly Disagree

1. Who will be responsible for deciding whether Workflow and Collaboration goes ahead or not after the initial investigations?
<--- Score

2. Do we say no to customers for no reason?
<--- Score

3. What is our question?
<--- Score

4. How do we engage the workforce, in addition to satisfying them?
<--- Score

5. How to deal with Workflow and Collaboration Changes?
<--- Score

6. Who Uses What?
<--- Score

7. Think of your Workflow and Collaboration project. what are the main functions?
<--- Score

8. In retrospect, of the projects that we pulled the plug on, what percent do we wish had been allowed to keep going, and what percent do we wish had ended earlier?
<--- Score

9. What current systems have to be understood and/or changed?
<--- Score

10. What trouble can we get into?
<--- Score

11. If you had to rebuild your organization without any traditional competitive advantages (i.e., no killer a technology, promising research, innovative product/service delivery model, etc.), how would your people have to approach their work and collaborate together in order to create the necessary conditions for success?
<--- Score

12. Are we making progress? and are we making progress as Workflow and Collaboration leaders?

<--- Score

13. Who will use it?

<--- Score

14. Is our strategy driving our strategy? Or is the way in which we allocate resources driving our strategy?

<--- Score

15. Have benefits been optimized with all key stakeholders?

<--- Score

16. Is there a limit on the number of users in Workflow and Collaboration ?

<--- Score

17. What are the business goals Workflow and Collaboration is aiming to achieve?

<--- Score

18. What stupid rule would we most like to kill?

<--- Score

19. What are internal and external Workflow and Collaboration relations?

<--- Score

20. Do we have the right people on the bus?

<--- Score

21. Who else should we help?

<--- Score

22. Whose voice (department, ethnic group, women, older workers, etc) might you have missed hearing from in your company, and how might you amplify this voice to create positive momentum for your business?
<--- Score

23. Are we changing as fast as the world around us?
<--- Score

24. What would have to be true for the option on the table to be the best possible choice?
<--- Score

25. How Do We Create Buy-in?
<--- Score

26. Why should we adopt a Workflow and Collaboration framework?
<--- Score

27. If we got kicked out and the board brought in a new CEO, what would he do?
<--- Score

28. Who do we want our customers to become?
<--- Score

29. How can we become more high-tech but still be high touch?
<--- Score

30. What potential megatrends could make our business model obsolete?
<--- Score

31. Who do we think the world wants us to be?
<--- Score

32. How are we doing compared to our industry?
<--- Score

33. Are there Workflow and Collaboration Models?
<--- Score

34. What is our competitive advantage?
<--- Score

35. Workflow and Collaboration Service Sales Supply Chain, Procurement, Distribution
<--- Score

36. Which criteria are used to determine which projects are going to be pursued or discarded?
<--- Score

37. What did we miss in the interview for the worst hire we ever made?
<--- Score

38. What is Tricky About This?
<--- Score

39. What do we do when new problems arise?
<--- Score

40. What new services of functionality will be implemented next with Workflow and Collaboration ?
<--- Score

41. What information is critical to our organization that our executives are ignoring?
<--- Score

42. Were lessons learned captured and communicated?
<--- Score

43. What will be the consequences to the stakeholder (financial, reputation etc) if Workflow and Collaboration does not go ahead or fails to deliver the objectives?
<--- Score

44. What kind of crime could a potential new hire have committed that would not only not disqualify him/her from being hired by our organization, but would actually indicate that he/she might be a particularly good fit?
<--- Score

45. What role does communication play in the success or failure of a Workflow and Collaboration project?
<--- Score

46. How will we know if we have been successful?
<--- Score

47. Are there any disadvantages to implementing Workflow and Collaboration? There might be some that are less obvious?
<--- Score

48. How will you know that the Workflow and Collaboration project has been successful?

<--- Score

49. What is the purpose of Workflow and Collaboration in relation to the mission?
<--- Score

50. What are your most important goals for the strategic Workflow and Collaboration objectives?
<--- Score

51. Why should people listen to you?
<--- Score

52. Which functions and people interact with the supplier and or customer?
<--- Score

53. Who are four people whose careers I've enhanced?
<--- Score

54. Is the impact that Workflow and Collaboration has shown?
<--- Score

55. What are strategies for increasing support and reducing opposition?
<--- Score

56. Who is going to care?
<--- Score

57. To whom do you add value?
<--- Score

58. Will there be any necessary staff changes (redundancies or new hires)?

<--- Score

59. Are we / should we be Revolutionary or evolutionary?
<--- Score

60. What are the long-term Workflow and Collaboration goals?
<--- Score

61. Why don't our customers like us?
<--- Score

62. Do you have an implicit bias for capital investments over people investments?
<--- Score

63. Did my employees make progress today?
<--- Score

64. How do we make it meaningful in connecting Workflow and Collaboration with what users do day-to-day?
<--- Score

65. What am I trying to prove to myself, and how might it be hijacking my life and business success?
<--- Score

66. What is the estimated value of the project?
<--- Score

67. How do senior leaders deploy your organizations vision and values through your leadership system, to the workforce, to key suppliers and partners, and to customers and

other stakeholders, as appropriate?
<--- Score

68. How do I stay inspired?
<--- Score

69. How do you determine the key elements that affect Workflow and Collaboration workforce satisfaction? how are these elements determined for different workforce groups and segments?
<--- Score

70. What management system can we use to leverage the Workflow and Collaboration experience, ideas, and concerns of the people closest to the work to be done?
<--- Score

71. Your reputation and success is your lifeblood, and Workflow and Collaboration shows you how to stay relevant, add value, and win and retain customers
<--- Score

72. Is Workflow and Collaboration dependent on the successful delivery of a current project?
<--- Score

73. Are we relevant? Will we be relevant five years from now? Ten?
<--- Score

74. Do we underestimate the customer's journey?
<--- Score

75. What is the craziest thing we can do?
<--- Score

76. How likely is it that a customer would recommend our company to a friend or colleague?
<--- Score

77. What are the gaps in my knowledge and experience?
<--- Score

78. What are all of our Workflow and Collaboration domains and what do they do?
<--- Score

79. What counts that we are not counting?
<--- Score

80. How can we incorporate support to ensure safe and effective use of Workflow and Collaboration into the services that we provide?
<--- Score

81. Is the Workflow and Collaboration organization completing tasks effectively and efficiently?
<--- Score

82. Why are Workflow and Collaboration skills important?
<--- Score

83. How do we keep the momentum going?
<--- Score

84. Are you satisfied with your current role? If not, what is missing from it?
<--- Score

85. In the past year, what have you done (or could you have done) to increase the accurate perception of this company/brand as ethical and honest?
<--- Score

86. How do we provide a safe environment -physically and emotionally?
<--- Score

87. Who sets the Workflow and Collaboration standards?
<--- Score

88. If no one would ever find out about my accomplishments, how would I lead differently?
<--- Score

89. If you were responsible for initiating and implementing major changes in your organization, what steps might you take to ensure acceptance of those changes?
<--- Score

90. Do we have the right capabilities and capacities?
<--- Score

91. How is business? Why?
<--- Score

92. What are the rules and assumptions my industry operates under? What if the opposite were true?
<--- Score

93. Political -is anyone trying to undermine this project?

<--- Score

94. Is maximizing Workflow and Collaboration protection the same as minimizing Workflow and Collaboration loss?
<--- Score

95. How important is Workflow and Collaboration to the user organizations mission?
<--- Score

96. Will it be accepted by users?
<--- Score

97. What is our Workflow and Collaboration Strategy?
<--- Score

98. Design Thinking: Integrating Innovation, Workflow and Collaboration Experience, and Brand Value
<--- Score

99. Do you have a vision statement?
<--- Score

100. Whom among your colleagues do you trust, and for what?
<--- Score

101. Will I get fired?
<--- Score

102. What one word do we want to own in the minds of our customers, employees, and partners?
<--- Score

103. How would our PR, marketing, and social media

change if we did not use outside agencies?
<--- Score

104. Who will manage the integration of tools?
<--- Score

105. What happens if you do not have enough funding?
<--- Score

106. What would I recommend my friend do if he were facing this dilemma?
<--- Score

107. How can you negotiate Workflow and Collaboration successfully with a stubborn boss, an irate client, or a deceitful coworker?
<--- Score

108. What are the short and long-term Workflow and Collaboration goals?
<--- Score

109. What are the usability implications of Workflow and Collaboration actions?
<--- Score

110. Who will determine interim and final deadlines?
<--- Score

111. Do we have enough freaky customers in our portfolio pushing us to the limit day in and day out?
<--- Score

112. Do we think we know, or do we know we

know ?
<--- Score

113. What are the challenges?
<--- Score

114. How will we build a 100-year startup?
<--- Score

115. What are the top 3 things at the forefront of our Workflow and Collaboration agendas for the next 3 years?
<--- Score

116. In what ways are Workflow and Collaboration vendors and us interacting to ensure safe and effective use?
<--- Score

117. Are the criteria for selecting recommendations stated?
<--- Score

118. How does Workflow and Collaboration integrate with other business initiatives?
<--- Score

119. What are specific Workflow and Collaboration Rules to follow?
<--- Score

120. How to Secure Workflow and Collaboration?
<--- Score

121. What is an unauthorized commitment?
<--- Score

122. Do you have any supplemental information to add to this checklist?

<--- Score

123. If we weren't already in this business, would we enter it today? And if not, what are we going to do about it?

<--- Score

124. Who is responsible for ensuring appropriate resources (time, people and money) are allocated to Workflow and Collaboration?

<--- Score

125. Are we paying enough attention to the partners our company depends on to succeed?

<--- Score

126. How do we ensure that implementations of Workflow and Collaboration products are done in a way that ensures safety?

<--- Score

127. Marketing budgets are tighter, consumers are more skeptical, and social media has changed forever the way we talk about Workflow and Collaboration. How do we gain traction?

<--- Score

128. What happens at this company when people fail?

<--- Score

129. Which Workflow and Collaboration goals are the most important?

<--- Score

130. Are new benefits received and understood?
<--- Score

131. Are assumptions made in Workflow and Collaboration stated explicitly?
<--- Score

132. If there were zero limitations, what would we do differently?
<--- Score

133. Who is responsible for errors?
<--- Score

134. What does your signature ensure?
<--- Score

135. How do we manage Workflow and Collaboration Knowledge Management (KM)?
<--- Score

136. How do we go about Securing Workflow and Collaboration?
<--- Score

137. What threat is Workflow and Collaboration addressing?
<--- Score

138. What are the critical success factors?
<--- Score

139. Who have we, as a company, historically been when we've been at our best?
<--- Score

140. What are we challenging, in the sense that Mac challenged the PC or Dove tackled the Beauty Myth?
<--- Score

141. Who are you going to put out of business, and why?
<--- Score

142. How will we insure seamless interoperability of Workflow and Collaboration moving forward?
<--- Score

143. Is there any reason to believe the opposite of my current belief?
<--- Score

144. What is the funding source for this project?
<--- Score

145. Do I know what I'm doing? And who do I call if I don't?
<--- Score

146. What are the Key enablers to make this Workflow and Collaboration move?
<--- Score

147. You may have created your customer policies at a time when you lacked resources, technology wasn't up-to-snuff, or low service levels were the industry norm. Have those circumstances changed?
<--- Score

148. Have new benefits been realized?

<--- Score

149. When information truly is ubiquitous, when reach and connectivity are completely global, when computing resources are infinite, and when a whole new set of impossibilities are not only possible, but happening, what will that do to our business?
<--- Score

150. What have we done to protect our business from competitive encroachment?
<--- Score

151. How much contingency will be available in the budget?
<--- Score

152. What may be the consequences for the performance of an organization if all stakeholders are not consulted regarding Workflow and Collaboration?
<--- Score

153. Is it economical; do we have the time and money?
<--- Score

154. What is it like to work for me?
<--- Score

155. What trophy do we want on our mantle?
<--- Score

156. Is a Workflow and Collaboration Team Work effort in place?
<--- Score

157. We picked a method, now what?
<--- Score

158. Who will provide the final approval of Workflow and Collaboration deliverables?
<--- Score

159. If our customer were my grandmother, would I tell her to buy what we're selling?
<--- Score

160. How much does Workflow and Collaboration help?
<--- Score

161. Operational - will it work?
<--- Score

162. If I had to leave my organization for a year and the only communication I could have with employees was a single paragraph, what would I write?
<--- Score

163. How can we become the company that would put us out of business?
<--- Score

164. Which individuals, teams or departments will be involved in Workflow and Collaboration?
<--- Score

165. What is our formula for success in Workflow and Collaboration ?
<--- Score

166. How will we ensure we get what we expected?
<--- Score

167. What is Effective Workflow and Collaboration?
<--- Score

168. How do we accomplish our long range Workflow and Collaboration goals?
<--- Score

169. What is the range of capabilities?
<--- Score

170. If we do not follow, then how to lead?
<--- Score

171. Who, on the executive team or the board, has spoken to a customer recently?
<--- Score

172. Who uses our product in ways we never expected?
<--- Score

173. Why is it important to have senior management support for a Workflow and Collaboration project?
<--- Score

174. Schedule -can it be done in the given time?
<--- Score

175. What is the mission of the organization?
<--- Score

176. Are the assumptions believable and

achievable?
<--- Score

177. Where is our petri dish?
<--- Score

178. What happens when a new employee joins the organization?
<--- Score

179. Do you see more potential in people than they do in themselves?
<--- Score

180. Am I failing differently each time?
<--- Score

181. Who is On the Team?
<--- Score

182. Who is the main stakeholder, with ultimate responsibility for driving Workflow and Collaboration forward?
<--- Score

183. Think about the kind of project structure that would be appropriate for your Workflow and Collaboration project. should it be formal and complex, or can it be less formal and relatively simple?
<--- Score

184. Is there any existing Workflow and Collaboration governance structure?
<--- Score

185. What is your BATNA (best alternative to a negotiated agreement)?

<--- Score

186. How do we maintain Workflow and Collaboration's Integrity?

<--- Score

187. How long will it take to change?

<--- Score

188. What are the Essentials of Internal Workflow and Collaboration Management?

<--- Score

189. What are the basics of Workflow and Collaboration fraud?

<--- Score

190. What is something you believe that nearly no one agrees with you on?

<--- Score

191. What should we stop doing?

<--- Score

192. How do we foster innovation?

<--- Score

193. Which models, tools and techniques are necessary?

<--- Score

194. Who are the key stakeholders?

<--- Score

195. Ask yourself: how would we do this work if we only had one staff member to do it?
<--- Score

196. Do you keep 50% of your time unscheduled?
<--- Score

197. Do Workflow and Collaboration rules make a reasonable demand on a users capabilities?
<--- Score

198. In a project to restructure Workflow and Collaboration outcomes, which stakeholders would you involve?
<--- Score

199. What are the success criteria that will indicate that Workflow and Collaboration objectives have been met and the benefits delivered?
<--- Score

200. How do we foster the skills, knowledge, talents, attributes, and characteristics we want to have?
<--- Score

201. Instead of going to current contacts for new ideas, what if you reconnected with dormant contacts--the people you used to know? If you were going reactivate a dormant tie, who would it be?
<--- Score

202. Would you rather sell to knowledgeable and informed customers or to uninformed customers?
<--- Score

203. Where can we break convention?
<--- Score

204. How Do We Know if We Are Successful?
<--- Score

205. What business benefits will Workflow and Collaboration goals deliver if achieved?
<--- Score

206. What is the overall business strategy?
<--- Score

207. What knowledge, skills and characteristics mark a good Workflow and Collaboration project manager?
<--- Score

208. Design Thinking: Integrating Innovation, Workflow and Collaboration, and Brand Value
<--- Score

209. If our company went out of business tomorrow, would anyone who doesn't get a paycheck here care?
<--- Score

210. What sources do you use to gather information for a Workflow and Collaboration study?
<--- Score

211. Has implementation been effective in reaching specified objectives?
<--- Score

212. Can we maintain our growth without

detracting from the factors that have contributed to our success?
<--- Score

213. What is a feasible sequencing of reform initiatives over time?
<--- Score

214. Among our stronger employees, how many see themselves at the company in three years? How many would leave for a 10 percent raise from another company?
<--- Score

215. How do we Lead with Workflow and Collaboration in Mind?
<--- Score

216. What will drive Workflow and Collaboration change?
<--- Score

217. What was the last experiment we ran?
<--- Score

Add up total points for this section:
_ _ _ _ _ = Total points for this section

Divided by: _ _ _ _ _ _ (number of statements answered) = _ _ _ _ _ _
Average score for this section

Transfer your score to the Workflow and Collaboration Index at the beginning of the Self-Assessment.

Workflow and Collaboration and Managing Projects, Criteria for Project Managers:

1.0 Initiating Process Group: Workflow and Collaboration

1. What were things that you did very well and want to do the same again on the next Workflow and Collaboration project?

2. When must it be done?

3. Were escalated issues resolved promptly?

4. During which stage of Risk planning are risks prioritized based on probability and impact?

5. What must be done?

6. Who are the Workflow and Collaboration project stakeholders?

7. What communication items need improvement?

8. Where must it be done?

9. How Will You Know You Did It?

10. Just how important is your work to the overall success of the Workflow and Collaboration project?

11. Based on your Workflow and Collaboration project communication management plan, what worked well?

12. How well did the chosen processes fit the needs of the Workflow and Collaboration project?

13. What are the inputs required to produce the deliverables?

14. What were things that you need to improve?

15. When will the Workflow and Collaboration project be done?

16. At which stage, in a typical Workflow and Collaboration project do stake holders have maximum influence?

17. What areas were overlooked on this Workflow and Collaboration project?

18. How Will You Do It?

19. What are the tools and techniques to be used in each phase?

20. How is each deliverable reviewed, verified, and validated?

1.1 Project Charter: Workflow and Collaboration

21. Why Outsource?

22. What are you striving to accomplish (measurable goal(s))?

23. What is the most common tool for helping define the detail?

24. Assumptions: What factors, for planning purposes, are you considering to be true?

25. Environmental Stewardship and Sustainability Considerations: What is the process that will be used to ensure compliance with the Environmental Stewardship Policy?

26. Why do you need to manage scope?

27. What are the assumptions?

28. What are you trying to accomplish?

29. Is time of the essence?

30. What is the business need?

31. Fit with other Products Compliments – Cannibalizes?

32. What are some examples of a business case?

33. What are the assigned resources?

34. Why have you chosen the aim you have set forth?

35. Review the general mission What system will be affected by the improvement efforts?

36. What does it need to do?

37. Why is it important?

38. Who Manages Integration?

39. Name and describe the elements that deal with providing the detail?

40. Is it an improvement over existing products?

1.2 Stakeholder Register: Workflow and Collaboration

41. Is Your Organization Ready for Change?

42. Who is Managing Stakeholder Engagement?

43. How Big is the Gap?

44. Who wants to talk about Security?

45. What & Why?

46. What are the major Workflow and Collaboration project milestones requiring communications or providing communications opportunities?

47. How will Reports Be Created?

48. How should employers make their voices heard?

49. Who are the stakeholders?

50. What opportunities exist to provide communications?

51. What is the power of the stakeholder?

52. How much influence do they have on the Workflow and Collaboration project?

1.3 Stakeholder Analysis Matrix: Workflow and Collaboration

53. Why do you care?

54. Are you working on the right risks?

55. Price, value, quality?

56. Could any of the organizations weaknesses seriously threaten development?

57. How are the threatened Workflow and Collaboration project targets being used?

58. Competitor intentions - various?

59. Are there different rules or organizational models for men and women?

60. Who is most dependent on the resources at stake?

61. Information and research?

62. What is the stakeholders power and status in relation to the Workflow and Collaboration project?

63. Who has not been involved up to now but should have been?

64. What is our Risk Management?

65. What is the organizations competitors doing?

66. What do you Evaluate?

67. What advantages do the organizations stakeholders have?

68. What coalitions might build around the issues being tackled?

69. Inoculations or payment to receive them?

70. Organizational Applicability?

71. How much do resources cost?

72. How affected by the problem(s)?

2.0 Planning Process Group: Workflow and Collaboration

73. Do the partners have sufficient financial capacity to keep up the benefits produced by the programme?

74. What do they need to know about the Workflow and Collaboration project?

75. To what extent do the intervention objectives and strategies of the Workflow and Collaboration project respond to the organizations plans?

76. What is involved in Workflow and Collaboration project scope management, and why is good Workflow and Collaboration project scope management so important on information technology Workflow and Collaboration projects?

77. What good practices or successful experiences or transferable examples have been identified?

78. What makes your Workflow and Collaboration project successful?

79. How well defined and documented are the Workflow and Collaboration project management processes you chose to use?

80. Will you be replaced?

81. To what extent and in what ways are the Workflow and Collaboration project contributing to progress

towards organizational reform?

82. How can you tell when you are done?

83. To what extent have the target population and participants made the activities their own, taking an active role in it?

84. What input will you be required to provide the Workflow and Collaboration project team?

85. If a task is partitionable, is this a sufficient condition to reduce the Workflow and Collaboration project duration?

86. If you are late, will anybody notice?

87. Product Breakdown Structure (PBS): what is the Workflow and Collaboration project result or product, and how should it look like, what are its parts?

88. How are IT Workflow and Collaboration projects different?

89. In what way has the Workflow and Collaboration project come up with innovative measures for problem-solving?

90. What is the difference between the early schedule and late schedule?

91. How will users learn how to use the deliverables?

92. What is the critical path for this Workflow and Collaboration project, and what is the duration of the critical path?

2.1 Project Management Plan: Workflow and Collaboration

93. Why Change?

94. Is there anything you would now do differently on your Workflow and Collaboration project based on past experience?

95. What are the deliverables?

96. Are there any windfall benefits that would accrue to the Workflow and Collaboration project sponsor or other parties?

97. What is the justification?

98. When is the Workflow and Collaboration project management plan created?

99. What are the training needs?

100. Do the proposed changes from the Workflow and Collaboration project include any significant risks to safety?

101. Do there need to be organizational changes?

102. Does the selected plan protect privacy?

103. What is Workflow and Collaboration project Scope Management?

104. What happened during the process that you found interesting?

105. What Went Wrong?

106. Where does all this information come from?

107. Is mitigation authorized or recommended?

108. What does management expect of PMs?

109. What goes into your Workflow and Collaboration project Charter?

110. Does the implementation plan have an appropriate division of responsibilities?

111. What should you drop in order to add something new?

2.2 Scope Management Plan: Workflow and Collaboration

112. Are updated Workflow and Collaboration project time & resource estimates reasonable based on the current Workflow and Collaboration project stage?

113. Do you have funding for Workflow and Collaboration project and product development, implementation and on-going support?

114. Is a PMO (Workflow and Collaboration project Management Office) in place and provide oversight to the Workflow and Collaboration project?

115. Are cause and effect determined for risks when they occur?

116. Is the schedule updated on a periodic basis?

117. Are the results of quality assurance reviews provided to affected groups & individuals?

118. Are trade-offs between accepting the risk and mitigating the risk identified?

119. Are all payments made according to the contract(s)?

120. Are Workflow and Collaboration project contact logs kept up to date?

121. Organizational unit (e.g., department, team, or

person) who will accept responsibility for satisfactory completion of the item?

122. Process Groups – where do Scope Management Processes fit in?

123. Do you have the reasons why the changes to the organizational systems and capabilities are required?

124. Is the Workflow and Collaboration project Sponsor clearly communicating the Business Case or rationale for why this Workflow and Collaboration project is needed?

125. Has the budget been baselined?

126. Are Vendor invoices audited for accuracy before payment?

127. Are risk triggers captured?

128. Has the organization done similar tasks before?

129. Do you keep stake holders informed?

130. Are changes in scope (deliverable commitments) agreed to by all affected groups & individuals?

131. Are there any scope changes proposed for the previously authorized Workflow and Collaboration project?

2.3 Requirements Management Plan: Workflow and Collaboration

132. Describe the process for rejecting the Workflow and Collaboration project requirements. Who has the authority to reject Workflow and Collaboration project requirements?

133. Are all the stakeholders ready for the transition into the user community?

134. Have stakeholders been instructed in the Change Control process?

135. Is the system software (non-operating system) new to the IT Workflow and Collaboration project team?

136. What performance metrics will be used?

137. Do you have an appropriate arrangement for meetings?

138. Do you have an agreed upon process for alerting the Workflow and Collaboration project Manager if a request for change in requirements leads to a product scope change?

139. Who will perform the analysis?

140. Do you have price sheets and a methodology for determining the total proposal cost?

141. Did you distinguish the scope of work the contractor(s) will be required to do?

142. What cost metrics will be used?

143. Is stakeholder risk tolerance an important factor for the requirements process in this Workflow and Collaboration project?

144. In case of software development; Should you have a test for each code module?

145. How will you develop the schedule of requirements activities?

146. How knowledgeable is the primary Stakeholder(s) in the proposed application area?

147. How will requirements be managed?

148. How do you know that you have done this right?

149. How will you communicate scheduled tasks to other team members?

150. Will you have access to stakeholders when you need them?

151. Will the contractors involved take full responsibility?

2.4 Requirements Documentation: Workflow and Collaboration

152. Who provides requirements?

153. Are there legal issues?

154. Basic work/Business process; high-level, what is being touched?

155. How does what is being described meet the business need?

156. What is your Elevator Speech?

157. What if the system wasn t implemented?

158. What images does it conjure?

159. What are the acceptance criteria?

160. What marketing channels do you want to use: e-mail, letter or sms?

161. If applicable; are there issues linked with the fact that this is an offshore Workflow and Collaboration project?

162. Can you Check System Requirements?

163. Have the benefits identified with the system being identified clearly?

164. What is a show stopper in the requirements?

165. Who is interacting with the system?

166. What will be the integration problems?

167. Can the requirement be changed without a large impact on other requirements?

168. Validity. Does the system provide the functions which best support the customer s needs?

169. What are current process problems?

170. Is the origin of the requirement clearly stated?

171. Is your Business Case still valid?

2.5 Requirements Traceability Matrix: Workflow and Collaboration

172. Why use a WBS?

173. Is there a requirements traceability process in place?

174. What percentage of Workflow and Collaboration projects are producing traceability matrices between requirements and other work products?

175. How will it affect the stakeholders personally in their career?

176. Will you use a Requirements Traceability Matrix?

177. What is the WBS?

178. How small is small enough?

179. Describe the process for approving requirements so they can be added to the traceability matrix and Workflow and Collaboration project work can be performed. Will the Workflow and Collaboration project requirements become approved in writing?

180. How Do you Manage Scope?

181. Do we have a clear understanding of all subcontracts in place?

182. What are the chronologies, contingencies,

consequences, criteria?

183. Why Do you Manage Scope?

2.6 Project Scope Statement: Workflow and Collaboration

184. Do you anticipate new stakeholders joining the Workflow and Collaboration project over time?

185. Are there completion/verification criteria defined for each task producing an output?

186. If you were to write a list of what should not be included in the scope statement, what are some of the things that you would recommend be described as out-of-scope?

187. What is the product of this Workflow and Collaboration project?

188. Is there an information system for the Workflow and Collaboration project?

189. What is a process you might recommend to verify the accuracy of the research deliverable?

190. Is the scope of your Workflow and Collaboration project well defined?

191. Change Management vs. Change Leadership - What's the Difference?

192. Which Risks Does the Workflow and Collaboration project Focus On?

193. Will you need a statement of work?

194. Is the plan for the organization of the Workflow and Collaboration project resources adequate?

195. Is the Workflow and Collaboration project Sponsor function identified and defined?

196. Is the Workflow and Collaboration project organization documented and on file?

197. Have the Configuration Management functions been assigned?

198. Have the reports to be produced, distributed, and filed been defined?

199. What Went Right?

200. Are the meetings set up to have assigned note takers that will add action/issues to the issue list?

201. Does the scope statement still need some clarity?

2.7 Assumption and Constraint Log: Workflow and Collaboration

202. What does an audit system look like?

203. Does the traceability documentation describe the tool and/or mechanism to be used to capture traceability throughout the life cycle?

204. Is there adequate stakeholder participation for the vetting of requirements definition, changes and management?

205. Are requirements management tracking tools and procedures in place?

206. How can you prevent/fix violations?

207. No superfluous information or marketing narrative?

208. What do you log?

209. Would known impacts serve as impediments?

210. What is positive about the current process?

211. Diagrams and tables are included to explain complex concepts and increase overall readability?

212. How do you design an auditing system?

213. Are funding and staffing resource estimates

sufficiently detailed and documented for use in planning and tracking the Workflow and Collaboration project?

214. Is the process working, but people are not executing in compliance of the process?

215. Can you perform this task or activity in a more effective manner?

216. Are processes for release management of new development from coding and unit testing, to integration testing, to training, and production defined and followed?

217. What if failure during recovery?

218. What Weaknesses do you have?

219. How many Workflow and Collaboration project staff does this specific process affect?

220. What Threats might prevent us from getting there?

221. Contradictory information between document sections?

2.8 Work Breakdown Structure: Workflow and Collaboration

222. How Far Down?

223. When do you stop?

224. Is it a change in scope?

225. Is it still viable?

226. Why would you develop a Work Breakdown Structure?

227. How big is a work-package?

228. Is the Work breakdown Structure (WBS) defined and is the scope of the Workflow and Collaboration project clear with assigned deliverable owners?

229. Who has to do it?

230. Can you make it?

231. Do you need another level?

232. What is the probability of completing the Workflow and Collaboration project in less that xx days?

233. What is the probability that the Workflow and Collaboration project duration will exceed xx weeks?

234. Why is it useful?

235. How much detail?

236. How will you and your Workflow and Collaboration project team define the Workflow and Collaboration projects scope and work breakdown structure?

237. When would you develop a Work Breakdown Structure?

238. When does it have to be done?

239. Where does it take place?

240. What has to be done?

241. How many levels?

2.9 WBS Dictionary: Workflow and Collaboration

242. Are meaningful indicators identified for use in measuring the status of cost and schedule performance?

243. Does the contractors system identify work accomplishment against the schedule plan?

244. Does the accounting system provide a basis for auditing records of direct costs chargeable to the contract?

245. Major functional areas of contract effort?

246. Are the rates for allocating costs from each indirect cost pool to contracts updated as necessary to ensure a realistic monthly allocation of indirect costs without significant year-end adjustments?

247. Is subcontracted work defined and identified to the appropriate subcontractor within the proper WBS element?

248. Is undistributed budget limited to contract effort which cannot yet be planned to CWBS elements at or below the level specified for reporting to the Government?

249. Are indirect costs charged to the appropriate indirect pools and incurring organization?

250. Wbs elements contractually specified for reporting of status to us (lowest level only)?

251. Identify potential or actual overruns and underruns?

252. What is the goal?

253. Are the overhead pools formally and adequately identified?

254. How detailed should a Workflow and Collaboration project get?

255. Do work packages reflect the actual way in which the work will be done and are they meaningful products or management-oriented subdivisions of a higher level element of work?

256. Do the lines of authority for incurring indirect costs correspond to the lines of responsibility for management control of the same components of costs?

257. Are overhead budgets and costs being handled according to the disclosure statement when applicable, or otherwise properly classified (for example, engineering overhead, IR&D)?

258. Is future work which cannot be planned in detail subdivided to the extent practicable for budgeting and scheduling purposes?

259. Are data elements (BCWS, BCWP, and ACWP) progressively summarized from the detail level to the contract level through the CWBS?

260. Are all affected work authorizations, budgeting, and scheduling documents amended to properly reflect the effects of authorized changes?

2.10 Schedule Management Plan: Workflow and Collaboration

261. Are all activities captured and do they address all approved work scope in the Workflow and Collaboration project baseline?

262. Are the activity durations realistic and at an appropriate level of detail for effective management?

263. Can additional resources be added to subsequent tasks to reduce the durations of those tasks?

264. Is there a requirements change management processes in place?

265. Will the Workflow and Collaboration project sponsor be involved in preliminary schedule reviews?

266. Is the IMS used by all levels of management for Workflow and Collaboration project implementation and control?

267. What s the difference between % Complete and % work?

268. Is there an excessive and invalid use of task constraints and relationships of leads/lags?

269. Is an industry recognized mechanized support tool(s) being used for Workflow and Collaboration project scheduling & tracking?

270. Pareto diagrams, statistical sampling, flow charting or trend analysis used quality monitoring?

271. Is current scope of the Workflow and Collaboration project substantially different than that originally defined?

272. Are software metrics formally captured, analyzed and used as a basis for other Workflow and Collaboration project estimates?

273. Does a documented Workflow and Collaboration project organizational policy & plan (i.e. governance model) exist?

274. Has a provision been made to reassess Workflow and Collaboration project risks at various Workflow and Collaboration project stages?

275. Have the key functions and capabilities been defined and assigned to each release or iteration?

276. Have all unresolved risks been documented?

277. Are the predecessor and successor relationships accurate?

278. Has the scope management document been updated and distributed to help prevent scope creep?

279. Is a process defined to measure the performance of the schedule management process itself?

2.11 Activity List: Workflow and Collaboration

280. What is the organization s history in doing similar activities?

281. How should ongoing costs be monitored to try to keep the Workflow and Collaboration project within budget?

282. What is the least expensive way to complete the Workflow and Collaboration project within 40 weeks?

283. Where will it be performed?

284. Is infrastructure setup part of your Workflow and Collaboration project?

285. What is the total time required to complete the Workflow and Collaboration project if no delays occur?

286. Can you determine the activity that must finish, before this activity can start?

287. When do the individual activities need to start and finish?

288. What is the probability the Workflow and Collaboration project can be completed in xx weeks?

289. What are you counting on?

290. Who will perform the work?

291. In what sequence?

292. The WBS is developed as part of a Joint Planning session. But how do you know that youve done this right?

293. Is there anything planned that doesn t need to be here?

294. What will be performed?

295. What did not go as well?

296. What are the critical bottleneck activities?

297. What went well?

298. How do you determine the late start (LS) for each activity?

2.12 Activity Attributes: Workflow and Collaboration

299. Are the required resources available?

300. Activity: Whats In the Bag?

301. Is there a trend during the year?

302. Where else does it apply?

303. Resource is assigned to?

304. Can more resources be added?

305. Resources to accomplish the work?

306. Activity: Fair or Not Fair?

307. Are the required resources available or need to be acquired?

308. Does the organization of the data change its meaning?

309. Time for overtime?

310. How Do you Manage Time?

311. How many resources do you need to complete the work scope within a limit of X number of days?

312. How Much Activity Detail Is Required?

313. Whats the general pattern here?

314. How many days do you need to complete the work scope with a limit of X number of resources?

315. Have constraints been applied to the start and finish milestones for the phases?

316. Were there other ways you could have organized the data to achieve similar results?

2.13 Milestone List: Workflow and Collaboration

317. What would happen if a delivery of material was one week late?

318. What specific improvements did you make to the Workflow and Collaboration project proposal since the previous time?

319. New USPs?

320. Marketing - reach, distribution, awareness?

321. Sustaining internal capabilities?

322. How late can each activity be finished and started?

323. Reliability of data, plan predictability?

324. Effects on core activities, distraction?

325. Timescales, deadlines and pressures?

326. Who will manage the Workflow and Collaboration project on a day-to-day basis?

327. Environmental effects?

328. How late can the activity finish?

329. Usps (unique selling points)?

330. How soon can the activity start?

331. What has been done so far?

332. Level of the Innovation?

333. Global influences?

2.14 Network Diagram: Workflow and Collaboration

334. What controls the start and finish of a job?

335. What can be done concurrently?

336. What are the Key Success Factors?

337. Are you on time?

338. Are the Gantt Chart and/or Network Diagram updated periodically and used to assess the overall Workflow and Collaboration project timetable?

339. What are the tools?

340. What job or jobs could run concurrently?

341. Where Do Schedules Come From?

342. Will crashing x weeks return more in benefits than it costs?

343. What is the lowest cost to complete this Workflow and Collaboration project in xx weeks?

344. If a current contract exists, can you provide the vendor name, contract start, and contract expiration date?

345. If X is long, what would be the completion time if you break X into two parallel parts of y weeks and z

weeks?

346. If the Workflow and Collaboration project network diagram cannot change but you have extra personnel resources, what is the BEST thing to do?

347. Which type of network diagram allows you to depict four types of dependencies?

348. What is the probability of completing the Workflow and Collaboration project in less that xx days?

349. What must be completed before an activity can be started?

350. Review the logical flow of the network diagram. Take a look at which activities you have first and then sequence the activities. Do they make sense?

351. What are the Major Administrative Issues?

352. Planning: who, how long, what to do?

2.15 Activity Resource Requirements: Workflow and Collaboration

353. What are constraints that you might find during the Human Resource Planning process?

354. How many signatures do you require on a check and does this match what is in your policy and procedures?

355. Are there unresolved issues that need to be addressed?

356. Which logical relationship does the PDM use most often?

357. Do you use tools like decomposition and rolling-wave planning to produce the activity list and other outputs?

358. When does Monitoring Begin?

359. Other support in specific areas?

360. Anything else?

361. How do you handle petty cash?

362. What is the Work Plan Standard?

363. Why do you do that?

2.16 Resource Breakdown Structure: Workflow and Collaboration

364. What is the primary purpose of the human resource plan?

365. Why Time Management?

366. When do they need the information?

367. Who delivers the information?

368. Which resources should be in the resource pool?

369. What can you do to improve productivity?

370. The list could probably go on, but, the thing that you would most like to know is, How long & How much?

371. Who will use the system?

372. Who is allowed to see what data about which resources?

373. Who needs what information?

374. What Is Workflow and Collaboration project Communication Management?

375. How difficult will it be to do specific activities on this Workflow and Collaboration project?

376. Changes Based on Input from Stakeholders?

377. Why is this important?

378. Goals for the Workflow and Collaboration project. What is each stakeholders desired outcome for the Workflow and Collaboration project?

379. Why Do you Do It?

380. What are the requirements for resource data?

2.17 Activity Duration Estimates: Workflow and Collaboration

381. Do they make sense?

382. What type of people would you want on your team?

383. What type of activity sequencing method is required for these activities?

384. What is the BEST thing to do?

385. Is earned value analysis completed to assess Workflow and Collaboration project performance?

386. Do scope statements include the Workflow and Collaboration project objectives and expected deliverables?

387. What is the duration of a milestone?

388. Are risks monitored to determine if an event has occurred or if the mitigation was successful?

389. What is done after activity duration estimation?

390. Are steps identified by which Workflow and Collaboration project documents may be changed?

391. Do your results resemble a normal distribution?

392. Explanation Notice how many choices are half

right?

393. Research recruiting and retention strategies at three different companies. What distinguishes one company from another in this area?

394. What is the career outlook for Workflow and Collaboration project managers in information technology?

395. Briefly summarize the work done by Maslow, Herzberg, McClellan, McGregor, Ouchi, Thamhain and Wilemon, and Covey. How do their theories relate to Workflow and Collaboration project management?

396. What steps did the company take to earn this prestigious quality award?

397. How difficult will it be to complete specific activities on this Workflow and Collaboration project?

398. A Workflow and Collaboration project manager is using weighted average duration estimates to perform schedule network analysis. Which type of mathematical analysis is being used?

399. Are resource rates available to calculate Workflow and Collaboration project costs?

400. What is the difference between using brainstorming and the Delphi technique for risk identification?

2.18 Duration Estimating Worksheet: Workflow and Collaboration

401. Define the work as completely as possible. What work will be included in the Workflow and Collaboration project?

402. Value Pocket Identification & Quantification What Are Value Pockets?

403. What is the least expensive way to complete the Workflow and Collaboration project within 40 weeks?

404. Science = Process: Remember the Scientific Method?

405. Why estimate time and cost?

406. What info is needed?

407. What is the total time required to complete the Workflow and Collaboration project if no delays occur?

408. How should ongoing costs be monitored to try to keep the Workflow and Collaboration project within budget?

409. What work will be included in the Workflow and Collaboration project?

410. How can the Workflow and Collaboration project be displayed graphically to better visualize the

activities?

411. What does it mean to say a task is 75% complete after 3 months?

412. When does the organization expect to be able to complete it?

413. Do any colleagues have experience with the company and/or RFPs?

414. What is Cost and Workflow and Collaboration project Cost Management?

415. What utility impacts are there?

416. Is a Construction detail attached (to aid in explanation)?

417. Small or Large Workflow and Collaboration project?

418. For other activities, how much delay can be tolerated?

2.19 Project Schedule: Workflow and Collaboration

419. A master Workflow and Collaboration project schedule?

420. What documents, if any, will the subcontractor provide (eg Workflow and Collaboration project schedule, quality plan etc)?

421. How much slack is available in the Workflow and Collaboration project?

422. Are the original Workflow and Collaboration project schedule and budget realistic?

423. How closely did the initial Workflow and Collaboration project Schedule compare with the actual schedule?

424. What is Risk?

425. How effectively were issues able to be resolved without impacting the Workflow and Collaboration project Schedule or Budget?

426. How can you shorten the schedule?

427. What is the purpose of a Workflow and Collaboration project schedule?

428. Are there activities that came from a template or previous Workflow and Collaboration project that

are not applicable on this phase of this Workflow and Collaboration project?

429. How can you fix it?

430. Are key risk mitigation strategies added to the Workflow and Collaboration project schedule?

431. Why do you think schedule issues often cause the most conflicts on Workflow and Collaboration projects?

432. Did the Workflow and Collaboration project come in on schedule?

433. Was the Workflow and Collaboration project schedule reviewed by all stakeholders and formally accepted?

434. How detailed should a Workflow and Collaboration project get?

2.20 Cost Management Plan: Workflow and Collaboration

435. Were Workflow and Collaboration project team members involved in the development of activity & task decomposition?

436. Contractors scope – How will contractors scope be defined when contracts are let?

437. Cost management – How will the cost of changes be estimated and controlled?

438. What is Cost and Workflow and Collaboration project Cost Management?

439. Milestones – What are the key dates in executing the contract plan?

440. Are adequate resources provided for the quality assurance function?

441. Have Workflow and Collaboration project team accountabilities & responsibilities been clearly defined?

442. Is there an issues management plan in place?

443. Who should write the PEP?

444. Are assumptions being identified, recorded, analyzed, qualified and closed?

445. Is there a formal process for updating the Workflow and Collaboration project baseline?

446. Are estimating assumptions and constraints captured?

447. Does the Workflow and Collaboration project have a formal Workflow and Collaboration project Charter?

448. What is an Acceptance Management Process?

449. Is PERT / Critical Path or equivalent methodology being used?

450. Are target dates established for each milestone deliverable?

451. Is a PMO (Workflow and Collaboration project Management Office) in place and provide oversight to the Workflow and Collaboration project?

452. Cost tracking and performance analysis – How will cost tracking and performance analysis be accomplished?

453. Are software metrics formally captured, analyzed and used as a basis for other Workflow and Collaboration project estimates?

2.21 Activity Cost Estimates: Workflow and Collaboration

454. How do you do activity recasts?

455. What were things that you did very well and want to do the same again on the next Workflow and Collaboration project?

456. Why Do you Manage Cost?

457. Did the Workflow and Collaboration project team have the right skills?

458. Maintenance Reserve?

459. What areas were overlooked on this Workflow and Collaboration project?

460. Are cost subtotals needed?

461. How difficult will it be to do specific tasks on the Workflow and Collaboration project?

462. Who determines the quality and expertise of contractors?

463. Were the tasks or work products prepared by the consultant useful?

464. How many activities should you have?

465. Are data needed on characteristics of care?

466. Were you satisfied with the work?

467. What is the organization s history in doing similar tasks?

468. What is Procurement?

469. Estimated cost?

470. What is the activity inventory?

471. Based on your Workflow and Collaboration project communication management plan, what worked well?

472. Measurable - Are the targets measurable?

473. What areas does the group agree are the biggest success on the Workflow and Collaboration project?

2.22 Cost Estimating Worksheet: Workflow and Collaboration

474. What happens to any remaining funds not used?

475. What is the estimated labor cost today based upon this information?

476. Ask: are others positioned to know, are others credible, and will others cooperate?

477. What will others want?

478. What is the purpose of estimating?

479. Does the Workflow and Collaboration project provide innovative ways for stakeholders to overcome obstacles or deliver better outcomes?

480. Can a trend be established from historical performance data on the selected measure and are the criteria for using trend analysis or forecasting methods met?

481. What Can Be Included?

482. Identify the timeframe necessary to monitor progress and collect data to determine how the selected measure has changed?

483. Is it feasible to establish a control group arrangement?

484. Will the Workflow and Collaboration project collaborate with the local community and leverage resources?

485. How will the results be shared and to whom?

486. Is the Workflow and Collaboration project responsive to community need?

487. What additional Workflow and Collaboration project(s) could be initiated as a result of this Workflow and Collaboration project?

488. Who is best positioned to know and assist in identifying such factors?

489. What costs are to be estimated?

2.23 Cost Baseline: Workflow and Collaboration

490. How accurate do cost estimates need to be?

491. Have all approved changes to the cost baseline been identified and impact on the Workflow and Collaboration project documented?

492. How likely is it to go wrong?

493. When should cost estimates be developed?

494. Has the Workflow and Collaboration project documentation been archived or otherwise disposed as described in the Workflow and Collaboration project communication plan?

495. How long are you willing to wait before you find out were late?

496. What is it ?

497. Workflow and Collaboration project Goals -should others be reconsidered?

498. Has the actual cost of the Workflow and Collaboration project (or Workflow and Collaboration project phase) been tallied and compared to the approved budget?

499. Should a more thorough impact analysis be conducted?

500. Are procedures defined by which the cost baseline may be changed?

501. Does the suggested change request seem to represent a necessary enhancement to the product?

502. What is the consequence?

503. Are you asking management for something as a result of this update?

504. Is there anything unique in this Workflow and Collaboration project s scope statement that will affect resources?

505. Does the suggested change request represent a desired enhancement to the products functionality?

2.24 Quality Management Plan: Workflow and Collaboration

506. Are there procedures in place to effectively manage interdependencies with other Workflow and Collaboration projects / systems?

507. Is there a Quality Management Plan?

508. Results Available?

509. Sampling Part of Task?

510. How does your organization perform analyses to assess overall organizational performance and set priorities?

511. Are formal code reviews conducted?

512. How do you decide what information to record?

513. How do your action plans support the strategic objectives?

514. Who is Responsible for Writing the QAPP?

515. Who gets results of work?

516. What is the return on investment?

517. How do you decide what information needs to be recorded?

518. Meet how often?

519. How are calibration records kept?

520. Methodology followed?

521. Is there a Steering Committee in place?

522. How long do you retain data?

2.25 Quality Metrics: Workflow and Collaboration

523. Has it met internal or external standards?

524. What is the benchmark?

525. Is material complete (and does it meet the standards)?

526. What does this tell us?

527. Do the operators focus on determining; is there anything I need to worry about?

528. What if the biggest risk to your business were those people who dont complain?

529. Where is Quality Now?

530. What metrics are important and most beneficial to measure?

531. Has trace of defects been initiated?

532. How do you know if everyone is trying to improve the right things?

533. Are quality metrics defined?

534. Are there already quality metrics available that detect nonlinear embeddings and trends similar to the users perception?

535. How do you measure?

536. Was the overall quality better or worse than previous products?

537. What happens if you get an abnormal result?

538. Who notifies stakeholders of normal and abnormal results?

539. What approved evidence based screening tools can be used?

540. How are requirements conflicts resolved?

541. Have risk areas been identified?

542. Is a risk containment plan in place?

2.26 Process Improvement Plan: Workflow and Collaboration

543. What Is the Test-Cycle Concept?

544. Has the time line required to move measurement results from the points of collection to databases or users been established?

545. To elicit goal statements, do you ask a question such as, What do you want to achieve?

546. Why do you want to achieve the goal?

547. Purpose of Goal: The motive is determined by asking, Why do I want to achieve this goal?

548. Have storage and access mechanisms and procedures been determined?

549. If a Process Improvement Framework Is Being Used, Which Elements Will Help the Problems and Goals Listed?

550. What is quality and how will you ensure it?

551. How Do you Manage Quality?

552. Modeling current processes is great, but will you ever see a return on that investment?

553. The motive is determined by asking, Why do I want to achieve this goal?

554. What makes people good SPI coaches?

555. Are you meeting the quality standards?

556. What Lessons Have you Learned So Far?

557. Has a process guide to collect the data been developed?

558. What personnel are the coaches for your initiative?

559. Why Quality Management?

560. Does our process ensure quality?

561. What personnel are the champions for the initiative?

2.27 Responsibility Assignment Matrix: Workflow and Collaboration

562. Are authorized changes being incorporated in a timely manner?

563. What Do You Need to Implement Earned Value Management?

564. What do you do when people dont respond?

565. No Rs: If a task has no one listed as Responsible, who is getting the job done?

566. Are the bases and rates for allocating costs from each indirect pool consistently applied?

567. Can the contractor substantiate work package and planning package budgets?

568. Changes in the overhead pool and/or organization structures?

569. How many hours by each staff member/rate?

570. Will too many Signing-off responsibilities delay the completion of the activity/deliverable?

571. Does each activity-deliverable have exactly one Accountable responsibility, so that accountability is clear and decisions can be made quickly?

572. Does a missing responsibility indicate that the

current Workflow and Collaboration project is not yet fully understood?

573. Does the contractors system include procedures for measuring the performance of critical subcontractors?

574. Are all authorized tasks assigned to identified organizational elements?

575. Identify potential or actual budget-based and time-based schedule variances?

576. Contemplated overhead expenditure for each period based on the best information currently available?

577. Does the contractor use objective results, design reviews and tests to trace schedule performance?

578. Changes in the nature of the overhead requirements?

2.28 Roles and Responsibilities: Workflow and Collaboration

579. What is working well within your organizations performance management system?

580. Who is responsible for implementation activities and where will the functions, roles and responsibilities be defined?

581. Do you take the time to clearly define roles and responsibilities on Workflow and Collaboration project tasks?

582. Implementation of actions: Who are the responsible units?

583. Authority: What areas/Workflow and Collaboration projects in your work do you have the authority to decide upon and act on those decisions?

584. Are the quality assurance functions and related roles and responsibilities clearly defined?

585. Have you ever been a part of this team?

586. What expectations were met?

587. Does our vision/mission support a culture of quality data?

588. Who is responsible for each task?

589. Does the team have access to and ability to use data analysis tools?

590. What should you do now to prepare yourself for a promotion, increased responsibilities or a different job?

591. What should you do now to prepare for your career 5+ years from now?

592. Key conclusions and recommendations: Are conclusions and recommendations relevant and acceptable?

593. Are our budgets supportive of a culture of quality data?

594. Influence: What areas of organizational decision making are you able to influence when you do not have authority to make the final decision?

595. Are governance roles and responsibilities documented?

596. How well did the Workflow and Collaboration project Team understand the expectations of specific roles and responsibilities?

597. Once the responsibilities are defined for the Workflow and Collaboration project, have the deliverables, roles and responsibilities been clearly communicated to every participant?

598. What should you do now to ensure that you are meeting all expectations of your current position?

2.29 Human Resource Management Plan: Workflow and Collaboration

599. Are people being developed to meet the challenges of the future?

600. Is the firm certified as a supplier, wholesaler, regular dealer, or manufacturer of such products/ supplies?

601. Were sponsors and decision makers available when needed outside regularly scheduled meetings?

602. How to convince employees that this is a necessary process?

603. Are change requests logged and managed?

604. How well does the company communicate?

605. Is the Workflow and Collaboration project Sponsor clearly communicating the Business Case or rationale for why this Workflow and Collaboration project is needed?

606. Have adequate resources been provided by management to ensure Workflow and Collaboration project success?

607. Is current scope of the Workflow and Collaboration project substantially different than that originally defined?

608. Has the Workflow and Collaboration project manager been identified?

609. Is it possible to track all classes of Workflow and Collaboration project work (e.g. scheduled, unscheduled, defect repair, etc.)?

610. Has a Workflow and Collaboration project Communications Plan been developed?

611. Are there checklists created to determine if all quality processes are followed?

612. Did the Workflow and Collaboration project team have the right skills?

613. Was the scope definition used in task sequencing?

614. Quality Assurance overheads?

615. Has the Workflow and Collaboration project scope been baselined?

2.30 Communications Management Plan: Workflow and Collaboration

616. Conflict Resolution -which method when?

617. Do you have members of your team responsible for certain stakeholders?

618. Do you then often overlook a key stakeholder or stakeholder group?

619. Are there too many who have an interest in some aspect of your work?

620. Who is involved as you identify stakeholders?

621. Who are the members of the governing body?

622. How will the person responsible for executing the communication item be notified?

623. How Did the Term Stakeholder Originate?

624. Which stakeholders can influence others?

625. Who is the stakeholder?

626. How is this initiative related to other portfolios, programs, or Workflow and Collaboration projects?

627. What is the political influence?

628. Do you feel a register helps?

629. Are the stakeholders getting the information others need, are others consulted, are concerns addressed?

630. Are there potential barriers between the team and the stakeholder?

631. Can you think of other people who might have concerns or interests?

632. What help do you and your team need from the stakeholder?

633. What are the interrelationships?

634. How often do you engage with stakeholders?

635. What is Workflow and Collaboration project Communications Management?

2.31 Risk Management Plan: Workflow and Collaboration

636. How is Implementation of Risk Actions Performed?

637. Was an original risk assessment/risk management plan completed?

638. Are there risks to human health or the environment that need to be controlled or mitigated?

639. Risk Categories: What are the main categories of risks that should be addressed on this Workflow and Collaboration project?

640. Is the technology to be built new to your organization?

641. Number of users of the product?

642. Is the process supported by tools?

643. What can you do to minimize the impact if it does?

644. Can it be changed quickly?

645. Technology risk: Is the Workflow and Collaboration project technically feasible?

646. Risk Documentation: What reporting formats and processes will be used for risk management activities?

647. Why do you want risk management?

648. What are the cost, schedule and resource impacts of avoiding the risk?

649. What can go wrong?

650. How is Risk Identification Performed?

651. Have customers been involved fully in the definition of requirements?

652. Market risk: Will the new product be useful to the organization or marketable to others?

653. Are end-users enthusiastically committed to the Workflow and Collaboration project and the system/product to be built?

654. Is Workflow and Collaboration project scope stable?

655. What other risks are created by choosing an avoidance strategy?

2.32 Risk Register: Workflow and Collaboration

656. Are our objectives at risk?

657. Which key risks have ineffective responses or outstanding improvement actions?

658. Are corrective measures implemented as planned?

659. When will it happen?

660. What is a Risk?

661. Why would you develop a risk register?

662. What could prevent us delivering on the strategic program objectives and what is being done to mitigate such issues?

663. Manageability – Have mitigations to the risk been identified?

664. What are you going to do to limit the Workflow and Collaboration projects risk exposure due to the identified risks?

665. Are implemented controls working as others should?

666. Can the likelihood and impact of failing to achieve such recommendations and action plans be

assessed?

667. What are the assumptions and current status that support the assessment of the risk?

668. What has changed since the last period?

669. Are there any knock-on effects/impact on any of the other areas?

670. Severity Prediction?

671. Having taken action, how did the responses effect change, and where is the Workflow and Collaboration project now?

672. Recovery actions - planned actions taken once a risk has occurred to allow you to move on. What should you do after?

673. What are the main aims, objectives of the policy, strategy, or service and the intended outcomes?

674. What can be done about it?

2.33 Probability and Impact Assessment: Workflow and Collaboration

675. How do you maximize short-term return on investment?

676. Do the people have the right combinations of skills?

677. Can the Workflow and Collaboration project proceed without assuming the risk?

678. Are people attending meetings and doing work?

679. Are there any Workflow and Collaboration projects similar to this one in existence?

680. How will economic events and trends likely affect the Workflow and Collaboration project?

681. Do you use any methods to analyze risks?

682. Is it necessary to deeply assess all Workflow and Collaboration project risks?

683. Are team members trained in the use of the tools?

684. What is the experience (performance, attitude, business ethics, etc.) in the past with contractors?

685. Have staff received necessary training?

686. What kind of preparation would be required to do this?

687. What should be the level of difficulty in handling the technology?

688. Is the number of people on the Workflow and Collaboration project team adequate to do the job?

689. Do you use diagramming techniques to show cause and effect?

690. What are the risks involved in appointing external agencies to manage the Workflow and Collaboration project?

691. Costs associated with late delivery or a defective product?

692. Do requirements put excessive performance constraints on the product?

693. Are the risk data complete?

2.34 Probability and Impact Matrix: Workflow and Collaboration

694. What will be the likely political situation during the life of the Workflow and Collaboration project?

695. Which role do you have in the Workflow and Collaboration project?

696. How can you understand and diagnose risks and identify sources?

697. What are the preparations required for facing difficulties?

698. Workarounds are determined during which risk management process?

699. Which should be probably done NEXT?

700. How should you structure risks?

701. What are ways to measure and evaluate risks?

702. Is the present organizational structure for handling the Workflow and Collaboration project sufficient?

703. Premium on reliability of product?

704. What should be the level of coordination?

705. Can it be enlarged by drawing people from other

areas of the organization?

706. What are the uncertainties associated with the technology selected for the Workflow and Collaboration project?

707. What will be the impact or consequence if the risk occurs?

708. How are you working with risks?

709. What should be done NEXT?

710. What is the likely future demand of the customer?

711. How to prioritize risks?

2.35 Risk Data Sheet: Workflow and Collaboration

712. What can happen?

713. Do effective diagnostic tests exist?

714. What is the environment within which you operate (social trends, economic, community values, broad based participation, national directions etc.)?

715. Risk of What?

716. What is the likelihood of it happening?

717. What is the duration of infection (the length of time the host is infected with the organizm) in a normal healthy human host?

718. During work activities could hazards exist?

719. What do people affected think about the need for, and practicality of preventive measures?

720. Potential for Recurrence?

721. Has a sensitivity analysis been carried out?

722. Are new hazards created?

723. What are you weak at and therefore need to do better?

724. What can YOU do?

725. Who has a vested interest in how you perform as an organization (our stakeholders)?

726. How reliable is the data source?

727. What are the main threats to our existence?

728. What were the Causes that contributed?

729. What will be the consequences if it happens?

730. Would you prefer an unknown or 70/30 chance?

731. Will revised controls lead to tolerable risk levels?

2.36 Procurement Management Plan: Workflow and Collaboration

732. Have activity relationships and interdependencies within tasks been adequately identified?

733. What areas are overlooked on this Workflow and Collaboration project?

734. Are issues raised, assessed, actioned, and resolved in a timely and efficient manner?

735. Have lessons learned been conducted after each Workflow and Collaboration project release?

736. Has a provision been made to reassess Workflow and Collaboration project risks at various Workflow and Collaboration project stages?

737. Are multiple estimation methods being employed?

738. Are quality inspections and review activities listed in the Workflow and Collaboration project schedule(s)?

739. Based on your Workflow and Collaboration project communication management plan, what worked well?

740. Have Workflow and Collaboration project team accountabilities & responsibilities been clearly

defined?

741. Are the people assigned to the Workflow and Collaboration project sufficiently qualified?

742. Have stakeholder accountabilities & responsibilities been clearly defined?

743. Specific - Is the objective clear in terms of what, how, when, and where the situation will be changed?

744. Alignment to strategic goals & objectives?

745. Sensitivity analysis?

746. Were Workflow and Collaboration project team members involved in the development of activity & task decomposition?

747. Has a capability assessment been conducted?

748. Are Workflow and Collaboration project team roles and responsibilities identified and documented?

749. Does all Workflow and Collaboration project documentation reside in a common repository for easy access?

2.37 Source Selection Criteria: Workflow and Collaboration

750. Are they compliant with all technical requirements?

751. Does your documentation identify why the team concurs or differs with reported performance from past performance report (CPARs, questionnaire responses, etc.)?

752. What management structure does the organization consider as optimal for performing the contract?

753. How will you evaluate offeror s proposals?

754. What Can Not Be Disclosed?

755. When is it appropriate to issue a DRFP?

756. What is cost analysis and when should it be performed?

757. Does the evaluation of any change include an impact analysis; how will the change affect the scope, time, cost, and quality of the goods or services being provided?

758. Who is on the Source Selection Advisory Committee?

759. What are Open Book debriefings?

760. What are the steps in performing a cost/tech tradeoff?

761. Can you make a cost/technical tradeoff?

762. What are the most critical evaluation criteria that prove to be tiebreakers in the evaluation of proposals?

763. What procedures are followed when a contractor requires access to classified information or a significant quantity of special material/information?

764. What documentation is necessary regarding electronic communications?

765. Is the offeror pricing what is technically proposed?

766. Team Leads: What is your process for assigning ratings?

767. What information may not be provided?

768. Is a cost realism analysis used?

769. What are the requirements for publicizing a RFP?

2.38 Stakeholder Management Plan: Workflow and Collaboration

770. Will all relevant stakeholders be included within the review process?

771. Are enough systems & user personnel assigned to the Workflow and Collaboration project?

772. Does the Business Case include how the Workflow and Collaboration project aligns with the organizations strategic goals & objectives?

773. Is Workflow and Collaboration project status reviewed with the steering and executive teams at appropriate intervals?

774. Are internal Workflow and Collaboration project status meetings held at reasonable intervals?

775. Are there any potential occupational health and safety issues due to the proposed purchases?

776. Are mitigation strategies identified?

777. Is the Steering Committee active in Workflow and Collaboration project oversight?

778. What action will be taken once reports have been received?

779. Have Workflow and Collaboration project team accountabilities & responsibilities been clearly

defined?

780. Is staff trained on the software technologies that are being used on the Workflow and Collaboration project?

781. Who will the report(s) be delivered to?

782. Are non-critical path items updated and agreed upon with the teams?

783. Has a Resource Management Plan been created?

784. Have adequate resources been provided by management to ensure Workflow and Collaboration project success?

2.39 Change Management Plan: Workflow and Collaboration

785. What are the specific target groups / audience that will be impacted by this change?

786. Who is the audience for change management activities?

787. What are the key change management success metrics?

788. Are there any restrictions on who can receive the communications?

789. What type of materials/channels will be available to leverage?

790. What are the responsibilities assigned to each role?

791. Is it the same for each of the business units?

792. Will a different work structure focus people on what is important?

793. What will be the preferred method of delivery?

794. What are the current methods of sharing information and do there need to be new ones developed?

795. Will all Field Readiness Criteria have been

practically met prior to training roll-out?

796. Who is responsible for which tasks?

797. Who should be involved in developing a change management strategy?

798. Is a training information sheet available?

799. What is the worst thing that can happen if you chose not to communicate this information?

800. Clearly articulate the overall business benefits of the Workflow and Collaboration project -why are you doing this now?

801. How will you deal with anger about the restricting of communications due to confidentiality considerations?

802. Have the business unit contacts been selected and notified?

803. What goal(s) do you hope to accomplish?

804. Who in the business it includes?

3.0 Executing Process Group: Workflow and Collaboration

805. What is the critical path for this Workflow and Collaboration project and how long is it?

806. Could a new application negatively affect the current IT infrastructure?

807. If a risk event occurs, what will you do?

808. How well did the chosen processes fit the needs of the Workflow and Collaboration project?

809. How well did the chosen processes produce the expected results?

810. What is in place for ensuring adequate change control on Workflow and Collaboration projects that involve outside contracts?

811. When do you share the scorecard with managers?

812. How could stakeholders negatively impact your Workflow and Collaboration project?

813. What Business Situation Is Being Addressed?

814. What are crucial elements of successful Workflow and Collaboration project plan execution?

815. What Workflow and Collaboration projects and

services are in the portfolio of your organization?

816. On which process should team members spend the most time?

817. Just how important is your work to the overall success of the Workflow and Collaboration project?

818. What are some crucial elements of a good Workflow and Collaboration project plan?

819. Do Workflow and Collaboration project managers understand the organizational context for their Workflow and Collaboration projects?

820. Will new hardware or software be required for servers or client machines?

821. How does a Workflow and Collaboration project life cycle differ from a product life cycle?

822. Does the case present a realistic scenario?

823. Would you rate yourself as being risk-averse, risk-neutral, or risk-seeking?

3.1 Team Member Status Report: Workflow and Collaboration

824. Are the attitudes of staff regarding Workflow and Collaboration project work improving?

825. How it is to be done?

826. Does the product, good, or service already exist within the organization?

827. When a teams productivity and success depend on collaboration and the efficient flow of information, what generally fails them?

828. Will the staff do training or is that done by a third party?

829. Is there evidence that staff is taking a more professional approach toward management of the organizations Workflow and Collaboration projects?

830. How will Resource Planning be done?

831. Are the products of the organization's Workflow and Collaboration projects meeting their customer's objectives?

832. Do you have an Enterprise Workflow and Collaboration project Management Office (EPMO)?

833. Why is it to be done?

834. How much risk is involved?

835. What is to be done?

836. How can you make it practical?

837. Does the organization have the means (staff, money, contract, etc.) to produce or to acquire the product, good, or service?

838. What specific interest groups do you have in place?

839. The problem with Reward & Recognition Programs is that the truly deserving people all too often get left out. How can you make it practical?

840. How does this product, good, or service meet the needs of the Workflow and Collaboration project and the organization as a whole?

841. Does every department have to have a Workflow and Collaboration project Manager on staff?

842. Are the organization's Workflow and Collaboration projects more successful over time?

3.2 Change Request: Workflow and Collaboration

843. What are the requirements for urgent changes?

844. When to Submit a Change Request?

845. What is the purpose of change control?

846. Screen shots or attachments included in a Change Request?

847. Have all related configuration items been properly updated?

848. Should staff call into the helpdesk or go to the website?

849. Will all change requests and current status be logged?

850. Are there requirements attributes that are strongly related to the complexity and size?

851. How is quality being addressed on the Workflow and Collaboration project?

852. Change Request Coordination ?

853. Has the change been highlighted and documented in the CSCI?

854. Why were my requested changes rejected or not

made?

855. How many times must the change be modified or presented to the change control board before it is approved?

856. What should be regulated in a change control operating instruction?

857. Are you Implementing ITIL Processes?

858. Can you answer what happened, who did it, when did it happen, and what else will be affected?

859. How to Get Changes (Code) Out in a Timely Manner?

860. How does a team identify the discrete elements of a configuration?

861. Who is included in the change control team?

862. Describe how modifications, enhancements, defects and/or deficiencies shall be notified (e.g. Problem Reports, Change Requests etc) and managed. Detail warranty and/or maintenance periods?

3.3 Change Log: Workflow and Collaboration

863. Is the submitted change a new change or a modification of a previously approved change?

864. Will the Workflow and Collaboration project fail if the change request is not executed?

865. Is the change request open, closed or pending?

866. How does this relate to the standards developed for specific business processes?

867. Is the requested change request a result of changes in other Workflow and Collaboration project(s)?

868. Who initiated the change request?

869. Where Do Changes Come From?

870. How does this change affect scope?

871. Is this a mandatory replacement?

872. Is the change request within Workflow and Collaboration project scope?

873. When was the request submitted?

874. Do the described changes impact on the integrity or security of the system?

875. Is the change backward compatible without limitations?

876. How does this change affect the timeline of the schedule?

877. When was the request approved?

3.4 Decision Log: Workflow and Collaboration

878. With whom was the decision shared or discussed?

879. How does provision of information, both in terms of content and presentation, influence acceptance of alternative strategies?

880. What eDiscovery problem or issue did your company set out to fix or make better?

881. How effective is maintaining the log at facilitating organizational learning?

882. Behaviors; what are guidelines that the team has identified that will assist them with getting the most out of their team meetings?

883. Who is the decisionmaker?

884. How does the use a Decision Support System influence the strategies/tactics or costs?

885. What makes you different or better than others companies selling the same thing?

886. Linked to original objective?

887. At what point in time does loss become unacceptable?

888. Is everything working as expected?

889. What is your overall strategy for quality control / quality assurance procedures?

890. So, what is the line where eDiscovery ends and document review begins?

891. Meeting purpose; why does this team meet?

892. How do you define success?

893. What alternatives/risks were considered?

894. Which variables make a critical difference?

895. Decision-making process; how will the team make decisions?

896. What are the cost implications?

897. Who will be given a copy of this document and where will it be kept?

3.5 Quality Audit: Workflow and Collaboration

898. How does the organization know that its staff financial services are appropriately effective and constructive?

899. How does the organization know that its system for managing intellectual property issues is appropriately effective, constructive and fair?

900. How does the organization know that its staffing profile is optimally aligned with the capability requirements implicit (or explicit) in its Strategic Plan?

901. What happens if our organization fails its Quality Audit?

902. Is there a written corporate quality policy?

903. How does the organization know that its management of its ethical responsibilities is appropriately effective and constructive?

904. Statements of intent remain exactly that until they are put into effect. The next step is to deploy those intentions. In other words, do the plans happen in reality?

905. How does the organization know that its staff entrance standards are appropriately effective and constructive and being implemented consistently?

906. How does the organization know that its staff have appropriate access to a fair and effective grievance process?

907. How does the organization know that its management system is appropriately effective and constructive?

908. Are there appropriate means for intervening if necessary?

909. How does the organization know that its information technology system is serving its needs as effectively and constructively as is appropriate?

910. Is progress against the intentions measurable?

911. What has changed/improved as a result of the review processes?

912. What does the organizarion look for in a Quality audit?

913. Are there sufficient personnel having the necessary education, background, training, and experience to assure that all operations are correctly performed?

914. How does the organization know that its methods are appropriately effective and constructive?

915. Are all complaints involving the possible failure of a device, labeling, or packaging to meet any of its specifications reviewed, evaluated, and investigated?

916. Are salvageable and salvaged medical devices

stored in a manner to prevent damage and/or contamination?

917. What does an analysis of an organizations staff profile suggest in terms of its planning, and how is this being addressed?

3.6 Team Directory: Workflow and Collaboration

918. When will you produce deliverables?

919. Is construction on schedule?

920. Process Decisions: Do invoice amounts match accepted work in place?

921. Timing: when do the effects of communication take place?

922. Process Decisions: Are contractors adequately prosecuting the work?

923. Process Decisions: Do job conditions warrant additional actions to collect job information and document on-site activity?

924. Process Decisions: How well was task order work performed?

925. Have you decided when to celebrate the Workflow and Collaboration projects completion date?

926. How do unidentified risks impact the outcome of the Workflow and Collaboration project?

927. Process Decisions: Are there any statutory or regulatory issues relevant to the timely execution of work?

928. Does a Workflow and Collaboration project team directory list all resources assigned to the Workflow and Collaboration project?

929. How will the team handle changes?

930. Who will write the meeting minutes and distribute?

931. Process Decisions: Which organizational elements and which individuals will be assigned management functions?

932. Who will be the stakeholders on your next Workflow and Collaboration project?

933. Process Decisions: Are all issues being addressed to the satisfaction of both parties within approximately 30 days from the time the issue is identified?

934. Who will talk to the customer?

935. Who are the Team Members?

936. Where will the product be used and/or delivered or built when appropriate?

3.7 Team Operating Agreement: Workflow and Collaboration

937. Are there more than two native languages represented by your team?

938. What are the boundaries (organizational or geographic) within which you operate?

939. Did you draft the meeting agenda?

940. What is Group Supervision?

941. Are there differences in access to communication and collaboration technology based on team member location?

942. What types of accommodations will be formulated and put in place for sustaining the team?

943. Do you ask one question at a time and wait 10 seconds for members to respond?

944. Do you post meeting notes and the recording (if used) and notify participants?

945. Do you listen for voice tone and word choice to understand the meaning behind words?

946. The method to be used in the decision making process; Will it be consensus, majority rule, or the supervisor having the final say?

947. Are team roles clearly defined and accepted?

948. What is Culture?

949. Do you ensure that all participants know how to use the required technology?

950. Do you ask participants to close their laptops and place their mobile devices on silent on the table while the meeting is in progress?

951. Do you call or email participants to ensure understanding, follow-through and commitment to the meeting outcomes?

952. Confidentiality: How will confidential information be handled?

953. Are leadership responsibilities shared among team members (versus a single leader)?

954. How does teaming fit in with overall organizational goals and meet organizational needs?

955. How will your group handle planned absences?

956. Must your members collaborate successfully to complete Workflow and Collaboration projects?

3.8 Team Performance Assessment: Workflow and Collaboration

957. Effects of crew composition on crew performance: Does the whole equal the sum of its parts?

958. To what degree do team members frequently explore the teams purpose and its implications?

959. When does the medium matter?

960. Which situations call for a more extreme type of adaptiveness in which team members actually re-define their roles?

961. To what degree will new and supplemental skills be introduced as the need is recognized?

962. Social categorization and intergroup behaviour: Does minimal intergroup discrimination make social identity more positive?

963. To what degree will the approach capitalize on and enhance the skills of all team members in a manner that takes into consideration other demands on members of the team?

964. To what degree does the teams work approach provide opportunity for members to engage in results-based evaluation?

965. Can familiarity breed backup?

966. To what degree can the team measure progress against specific goals?

967. To what degree are the goals ambitious?

968. To what degree are the skill areas critical to team performance present?

969. How hard do you try to make a good selection?

970. Individual task proficiency and team process behavior: Whats important for team functioning?

971. What are Teams?

972. To what degree are the relative importance and priority of the goals clear to all team members?

973. To what degree is the team cognizant of small wins to be celebrated along the way?

974. To what degree do all members feel responsible for all agreed-upon measures?

975. How do you recognize and praise members for their contributions?

976. If you have criticized someones work for method variance in your role as reviewer, what was the circumstance?

3.9 Team Member Performance Assessment: Workflow and Collaboration

977. How does your team work together?

978. Does the Rater (Supervisor) have the authority or responsibility to tell an employee that the employees performance is Unsatisfactory?

979. How should adaptive assessments be implemented?

980. To what degree are the teams goals and objectives clear, simple, and measurable?

981. What types of learning are targeted (e.g., cognitive, affective, psychomotor, procedural)?

982. How are performance measures and their associated incentives developed?

983. What stakeholders must be involved in the development and oversight of the performance plan?

984. To what extent are systems and applications (e.g., game engine, mobile device platform) utilized?

985. What are the staffs preferences for training on technology-based platforms?

986. For what period of time is a member rated?

987. To what degree do team members understand one anothers roles and skills?

988. How was the determination made for which training platforms would be used (i.e., media selection)?

989. Is There Reluctance to Join a Team?

990. What happens if a team member disagrees with the Job Expectations?

991. To what degree are the goals realistic?

992. Are any governance changes sufficient to impact achievement?

993. Who is responsible?

3.10 Issue Log: Workflow and Collaboration

994. Who needs to know and how much?

995. What approaches to you feel are the best ones to use?

996. How Do you Manage Communications?

997. What effort will a change need?

998. What is the stakeholders political influence?

999. What are the typical contents?

1000. Is access to the Issue Log controlled?

1001. Who is the issue assigned to?

1002. Which stakeholders are thought leaders, influences, or early adopters?

1003. What steps can you take for positive relationships?

1004. Are the stakeholders getting the information they need, are they consulted, are their concerns addressed?

1005. Are the Workflow and Collaboration project Issues uniquely identified, including to which product they refer?

1006. Why Do you Manage Human Resources?

1007. Are they needed?

1008. Which team member will work with each stakeholder?

4.0 Monitoring and Controlling Process Group: Workflow and Collaboration

1009. Is there undesirable impact on staff or resources?

1010. What are the goals of the program?

1011. A Workflow and Collaboration project management team of two has 8 key stakeholders to work with. How many potential communications channels exist on the Workflow and Collaboration project?

1012. Is the schedule for the set products being met?

1013. If no change, where should you look for problems?

1014. What resources are necessary?

1015. Is the verbiage used appropriate and understandable?

1016. How is Agile Program Management done?

1017. How will staff learn how to use the deliverables?

1018. Do the products created live up to the necessary quality?

1019. If action is called for, what form should it take?

1020. Accuracy: What design will lead to accurate information?

1021. What were things that you did very well and want to do the same again on the next Workflow and Collaboration project?

1022. What input will you be required to provide the Workflow and Collaboration project team?

1023. How is Agile Workflow and Collaboration project Management Done?

1024. Is progress on outcomes due to your program?

4.1 Project Performance Report: Workflow and Collaboration

1025. Next Steps?

1026. To what degree does the information network communicate information relevant to the task?

1027. To what degree do the relationships of the informal organization motivate task- relevant behavior and facilitate task completion?

1028. To what degree do members articulate the goals beyond the team membership?

1029. To what degree are the demands of the task compatible with and converge with the relationships of the informal organization?

1030.   To what degree can the cognitive capacity of individuals accommodate the flow of information?

1031. To what degree can team members vigorously define the team's purpose in discussions with others who are not part of the functioning team?

1032. To what degree does the funding match the requirement?

1033. To what degree will the team adopt a concrete, clearly understood, and agreed-upon approach that will result in achievement of the team's goals?

1034. To what degree do team members frequently explore the team's purpose and its implications?

1035. To what degree does the team's work approach provide opportunity for members to engage in results-based evaluation?

1036. How can Workflow and Collaboration project Sustainability be Maintained?

1037. To what degree do team members understand one another's roles and skills?

1038. To what degree does the formal organization make use of individual resources and meet individual needs?

1039. To what degree does the team's work approach provide opportunity for members to engage in open interaction?

4.2 Variance Analysis: Workflow and Collaboration

1040. What is the total budget for the Workflow and Collaboration project (including estimates for authorized but unpriced work)?

1041. What causes selling price variance?

1042. When, during the last four quarters, did a primary business event occur causing a fluctuation?

1043. The anticipated business volume?

1044. Are overhead cost budgets established for each department which has authority to incur overhead costs?

1045. How does your company measure performance?

1046. Are records maintained to show how undistributed budgets are controlled?

1047. Do the rates and prices remain constant throughout the year?

1048. Contemplated overhead expenditure for each period based on the best information currently is available?

1049. Wbs elements contractually specified for reporting of status to the organization (lowest level only)?

1050. What is your organizations rationale for sharing expenses and services between business segments?

1051. Are overhead costs budgets established on a basis consistent with the anticipated direct business base?

1052. Did a new competitor enter the market?

1053. Can Process Improvements Lead to Unfavorable Variances?

1054. Can the relationship with problem customers be restructured so that there is a win-win situation?

1055. Are management actions taken to reduce indirect costs when there are significant adverse variances?

1056. What is the actual cost of work performed?

1057. Did an existing competitor change their strategy?

4.3 Earned Value Status: Workflow and Collaboration

1058. Earned Value can be used in almost any Workflow and Collaboration project situation and in almost any Workflow and Collaboration project environment. It may be used on large Workflow and Collaboration projects, medium sized Workflow and Collaboration projects, tiny Workflow and Collaboration projects (in cut-down form), complex and simple Workflow and Collaboration projects and in any market sector. Some people, of course, know all about earned value, they have used it for years - but perhaps not as effectively as they could have?

1059. How much is it going to cost by the finish?

1060. What is the unit of forecast value?

1061. Verification is a process of ensuring that the developed system satisfies the stakeholders agreements and specifications; Are you building the product right? What do you verify?

1062. Where is Evidence-based Earned Value in your organization reported?

1063. Are you hitting your Workflow and Collaboration projects targets?

1064. How does this compare with other Workflow and Collaboration projects?

1065. Validation is a process of ensuring that the developed system will actually achieve the stakeholders desired outcomes; Are you building the right product? What do you validate?

1066. When is it going to finish?

1067. If earned value management (EVM) is so good in determining the true status of a Workflow and Collaboration project and Workflow and Collaboration project its completion, why is it that hardly any one uses it in information systems related Workflow and Collaboration projects?

1068. Where are your problem areas?

4.4 Risk Audit: Workflow and Collaboration

1069. Does your organization have a social media policy and procedure?

1070. Is your organization an exempt employer for payroll tax purposes?

1071. How do you compare to other jurisdictions when managing the risk of ....?

1072. Is Risk an management agenda item?

1073. Who is responsible for what?

1074. Are you willing to seek legal advice when required?

1075. Are there any forms the staff is required to sign?

1076. If applicable; Which route/packaging option do you choose for transport of hazmat material?

1077. Are the software tools integrated with each other?

1078. Risks with Workflow and Collaboration projects or new initiatives?

1079. Is Workflow and Collaboration project scope stable?

1080. What resources are needed to achieve program results?

1081. When your organization is entering into a major contract, does it seek legal advice?

1082. What can be measured?

1083. Are requirements fully understood by the team and their customers?

1084. Is a software Workflow and Collaboration project management tool available?

1085. Do you have written and signed agreements/ contracts in place for each paid staff member?

1086. Are procedures in place to ensure the security of staff and information and compliance with privacy legislation if applicable?

1087. Who audits the auditor?

1088. Is all required equipment available?

4.5 Contractor Status Report: Workflow and Collaboration

1089. What was the budget or estimated cost for your companys services?

1090. How is Risk Transferred?

1091. What process manages the contracts?

1092. Who can list a Workflow and Collaboration project as company experience, the company or a previous employee of the company?

1093. What was the final actual cost?

1094. How does the proposed individual meet each requirement?

1095. How long have you been using the services?

1096. If applicable; describe your standard schedule for new software version releases. Are new software version releases included in the standard maintenance plan?

1097. What was the actual budget or estimated cost for your companys services?

1098. Are there contractual transfer concerns?

1099. What are the minimum and optimal bandwidth requirements for the proposed soluiton?

1100. What is the average response time for answering a support call?

1101. What was the overall budget or estimated cost?

1102. Describe how often regular updates are made to the proposed solution. Are these regular updates included in the standard maintenance plan?

4.6 Formal Acceptance: Workflow and Collaboration

1103. Did the Workflow and Collaboration project achieve its MOV?

1104. What was done right?

1105. Does it do what Workflow and Collaboration project team said it would?

1106. Do you buy-in installation services?

1107. Did the Workflow and Collaboration project manager and team act in a professional and ethical manner?

1108. Have all comments been addressed?

1109. What function(s) does it fill or meet?

1110. Was the Workflow and Collaboration project goal achieved?

1111. What are the requirements against which to test, Who will execute?

1112. How well did the team follow the methodology?

1113. Is formal acceptance of the Workflow and Collaboration project product documented and distributed?

1114. Was business value realized?

1115. Was the client satisfied with the Workflow and Collaboration project results?

1116. Who supplies data?

1117. Who would use it?

1118. Does it do what client said it would?

1119. What features, practices, and processes proved to be strengths or weaknesses?

1120. How does your team plan to obtain formal acceptance on your Workflow and Collaboration project?

1121. Was the Workflow and Collaboration project work done on time, within budget, and according to specification?

1122. Do you perform formal acceptance or burn-in tests?

5.0 Closing Process Group: Workflow and Collaboration

1123. What were things that you did well, but could improve, and how?

1124. Just how important is your work to the overall success of the Workflow and Collaboration project?

1125. How well defined and documented were the Workflow and Collaboration project management processes you chose to use?

1126. Did you do things well?

1127. What is the Workflow and Collaboration project Management Process?

1128. What is the risk of failure to the organization?

1129. What is an Encumbrance?

1130. Mitigate. What will you do to minimize the impact should a risk event occur?

1131. Was the schedule met?

1132. How critical is the Workflow and Collaboration project success to the success of the organization?

1133. What were things that you did very well and want to do the same again on the next Workflow and Collaboration project?

1134. What could be done to improve the process?

1135. Who are the Workflow and Collaboration project stakeholders?

1136. Were decisions made in a timely manner?

5.1 Procurement Audit: Workflow and Collaboration

1137. Is the purchasing department facility laid out to facilitate interviews with salespersons?

1138. When you set social or environmental conditions for the performance of the contract, were these compatible with the law and was adequate information given to the candidates?

1139. When tenders were actually rejected because they were abnormally low, were reasons for this decision given and were they sufficiently grounded?

1140. Are all purchase orders reviewed by someone other than the individual preparing the purchase order (reasonableness of order and vendor selection)?

1141. Is the performance of the procurement function/unit benchmarked with other procurement functions/units in the different stages of the procurement process?

1142. What is the process cost of the procurement function?

1143. Are regulations and protective measures in place to avoid corruption?

1144. Are contract changes after awarding properly justified and executed?

1145. Are all purchase orders cancelled after payment to avoid duplicate payment of the same invoice?

1146. Is the organization transparent about winning bids and prices?

1147. Are review meetings organized during contract execution and do they meet demand?

1148. Are proper financing arrangements taken?

1149. Is the minutes book kept current?

1150. Have late payment interests been rewarded and could they have been avoided?

1151. Are risks managed to provide reasonable assurance regarding department procurement objectives?

1152. Is there a formal program of inservice training for personnel in the business management function?

1153. Where required, were candidates registered as approved contractors, suppliers or service providers or certified by relevant bodies?

1154. Are cases of double payment duly prevented and corrected?

1155. Is the functioning of automatic disbursement programs tested by an independent party?

1156. Are there mechanisms for evaluating the departments suppliers performance in relation to prices, quality, delivery and innovation?

5.2 Contract Close-Out: Workflow and Collaboration

1157. Was the contract sufficiently clear so as not to result in numerous disputes and misunderstandings?

1158. What happens to the recipient of services?

1159. Has each contract been audited to verify acceptance and delivery?

1160. A change in circumstances?

1161. How does it work?

1162. Parties: Authorized?

1163. How/When Used ?

1164. Are the signers the authorized officials?

1165. Have all acceptance criteria been met prior to final payment to contractors?

1166. A change in knowledge?

1167. Have all contracts been closed?

1168. Have all contract records been included in the Workflow and Collaboration project archives?

1169. Have all contracts been completed?

1170. Parties: Who is Involved?

1171. How is the contracting office notified of the automatic contract close-out?

1172. Was the contract type appropriate?

1173. A change in attitude or behavior?

1174. Was the contract complete without requiring numerous changes and revisions?

1175. What is Capture Management?

5.3 Project or Phase Close-Out: Workflow and Collaboration

1176. What Security Considerations needed to be addressed during the Procurement Life Cycle?

1177. What is this stakeholder expecting?

1178. What advantages do the an individual interview have over a group meeting, and vice-versa?

1179. Have business partners been involved extensively, and what data was required for them?

1180. What were the goals and objectives of the communications strategy for the Workflow and Collaboration project?

1181. What benefits or impacts does the stakeholder group expect to obtain as a result of the Workflow and Collaboration project?

1182. Which changes might a stakeholder be required to make as a result of the Workflow and Collaboration project?

1183. Can the lesson learned be replicated?

1184. Is the lesson based on actual Workflow and Collaboration project experience rather than on independent research?

1185. What was the preferred delivery mechanism?

1186. Was the user/client satisfied with the end product?

1187. How often did each stakeholder need an update?

1188. What process was planned for managing issues/ risks?

1189. Who exerted influence that has positively affected or negatively impacted the Workflow and Collaboration project?

1190. Is the lesson significant, valid, and applicable?

1191. What are the marketing communication needs for each stakeholder?

1192. What are they?

1193. What was learned?

5.4 Lessons Learned: Workflow and Collaboration

1194. How to Write Up the Lesson Identified – How will you document the results of your analysis such that you have an LI ready to take the next step in the LL process?

1195. Does the lesson describe a function that would be done differently the next time?

1196. How well did the Workflow and Collaboration project Manager respond to questions or comments related to the Workflow and Collaboration project?

1197. How objective was the collection of data?

1198. Did the Workflow and Collaboration project improve the team members reputations, skills, personal development?

1199. Was any formal risk assessment carried out at the start of the Workflow and Collaboration project, and was this followed up during the Workflow and Collaboration project?

1200. How did the estimated Workflow and Collaboration project Budget compare with the total actual expenditures?

1201. What were the most significant issues on this Workflow and Collaboration project?

1202. What should have been accomplished during predeployment that was not accomplished?

1203. How effective were Workflow and Collaboration project audits?

1204. Is there a clear cause and effect between the activity and the lesson learned?

1205. How effective was the support you received during implementation of the product/service?

1206. How actively and meaningfully were stakeholders involved in the Workflow and Collaboration project?

1207. How clear were you on your role in the Workflow and Collaboration project?

1208. How well were your expectations met regarding the extent of your involvement in the Workflow and Collaboration project (effort, time commitments, etc.)?

1209. Was sufficient advance training conducted and/or information provided to enable those affected by the changes to adjust to and accommodate them?

1210. Whom to share Lessons Learned Information with?

1211. How well did the scope of the Workflow and Collaboration project match what was defined in the Workflow and Collaboration project Proposal?

1212. What were the problems encountered in the

Workflow and Collaboration project-functional area relationship, why, and how could they be fixed?

Index

ability 32, 59, 170
abnormal   164
abnormally   232
absences   209
accept   118
acceptable   43, 67, 170
acceptance   6, 90, 121, 154, 201, 228-229, 234
accepted   91, 152, 206, 209
accepting   117
access 2, 9-10, 42-43, 120, 165, 170, 186, 188, 204, 208, 214
accomplish   8, 64, 99, 108, 138, 192
according   25, 117, 132, 229
account   11, 33
accounted   38
accounting   131
accrue 115
accuracy   46, 118, 125, 217
accurate   10, 90, 135, 159, 217
achievable   100
achieve   8, 50, 60, 67, 82, 139, 165, 177, 223, 225, 228
achieved   21, 67, 103, 228
acquire   196
acquired   138
across 40, 77
action 74, 77, 126, 161, 177-178, 189, 216
actionable   39
actioned   185
actions 22, 71, 92, 169, 175, 177-178, 206, 221
active 114, 189
actively   239
activities   21, 67, 74, 78, 114, 120, 134, 136-137, 140, 143,
145, 147-148, 150-151, 155, 169, 175, 183, 185, 191
activity 3-4, 30, 34, 128, 134, 136-138, 140-141, 143-144, 147, 153,
155-156, 167, 185-186, 206, 239
actual 34, 132, 151, 159, 168, 221, 226, 236, 238
actually   25, 59, 61, 76, 85, 210, 223, 232
adaptive   212
addition   9, 81
additional   26, 50-52, 55, 134, 158, 206
additions   70

address   21, 62, 134
addressed   144, 174-175, 193, 197, 205, 207, 214, 228, 236
addressing   32, 95
adequate   126-127, 153, 171, 180, 190, 193, 232
adequately   26, 45, 132, 185, 206
adjust 239
adopters   214
advance   239
advantage   49, 84
advantages   81, 112, 236
adverse   221
advice 224-225
advise 9
Advisory   187
affect 48, 53, 88, 123, 128, 160, 179, 187, 193, 199-200
affected   109, 112, 117-118, 133, 183, 198, 237, 239
affecting   13, 18, 52
affective   212
against28, 75, 77, 131, 204, 211, 228
agencies   92, 180
agenda   208, 224
agendas   93
Aggregate   40
agreed   45-46, 118-119, 190
Agreement   6, 101, 208
agreements   222, 225
agrees 101
aiming 82
alerting   119
alerts   71
aligned   20, 203
Alignment   186
aligns   189
alleged   1
allocate   82
allocated   94
allocating   131, 167
allocation   131
allowed   81, 145
allows 10, 143
almost 222
already   94, 163, 195
always 10

Amazon   11
ambitious   211
amended   133
America   24
amounts   206
amplify 55, 83
analyses   161
analysis   3, 6, 12, 36-37, 41, 43-46, 49, 51-53, 55, 60, 64, 67,
111, 119, 135, 147-148, 154, 157, 159, 170, 183, 186-188, 205, 220,
238
analyze   2, 37, 44, 46, 48, 51-52, 66, 179
analyzed   38, 41-43, 45, 47, 65, 71, 135, 153-154
another   11, 104, 129, 148, 219
anothers   213
answer 12-13, 17, 24, 35, 48, 57, 69, 80, 198
answered   23, 34, 47, 56, 68, 79, 104
answering   12, 227
anticipate   125
anybody   114
anyone   27, 90, 103
anything   115, 137, 144, 160, 163
appear   1
applicable   13, 121, 132, 152, 224-226, 237
applied   78, 139, 167
appointed   32-33
appointing   180
approach   42, 81, 195, 210, 218-219
approaches   59, 67, 214
approval   33, 98
approved   123, 134, 159, 164, 198-200, 233
approving   123
Architects   8
archived   159
archives   234
around 83, 112
articulate   192, 218
asking 1, 8, 160, 165
aspect 173
assess 18, 142, 147, 161, 179
assessed   178, 185
assessing   63, 72
Assessment   5-6, 9-10, 18, 175, 178-179, 186, 210, 212, 238
assign 22

assigned 31, 33, 109, 126, 129, 135, 138, 168, 186, 189, 191, 207, 214
assigning 188
Assignment 4, 167
assist 66, 158, 201
assistant 8
associated 180, 182, 212
assuming 179
Assumption 3, 127
assurance 117, 153, 169, 172, 202, 233
assure 45, 65, 204
attached 150
attainable 29
attempted 27
attempting 70
attendance 33
attendant 66
attended 33
attending 179
attention 13, 94
attitude 179, 235
attitudes 195
attributes 3, 102, 138, 197
audience 191
audited 118, 234
auditing 20, 69, 127, 131
auditor 225
auditors 62
audits 225, 239
auspices 9
author 1
authority 119, 132, 169-170, 212, 220
authorized 116, 118, 133, 167-168, 220, 234
automatic 233, 235
available 19, 22, 26, 31, 39, 50-51, 97, 138, 148, 151, 161, 163, 168, 171, 191-192, 220, 225
Average 13, 23, 34, 47, 56, 68, 79, 104, 148, 227
avoidance 176
avoided 233
avoiding 176
awarding 232
awareness 140
background 11, 204

backup   210
backward   200
balance   45
bandwidth   226
barriers 42, 174
baseline   4, 45, 134, 154, 159-160
baselined   40, 118, 172
baselines   31-32
basics 101
Beauty 96
because   42-43, 232
become   83, 98, 123, 201
before 10, 27, 77, 118, 136, 143, 159, 198
beginning   2, 16, 23, 34, 47, 56, 68, 79, 104
begins 202
behavior   211, 218, 235
Behaviors   42, 201
behaviour   210
behind 208
belief   12, 17, 24, 35, 48, 57, 69, 80, 96
believable   99
believe 96, 101
benchmark   163
beneficial   163
benefit 1, 19, 21, 60, 78
benefits   19, 50, 53, 80, 82, 95-96, 102-103, 113, 115, 121,
142, 192, 236
better 8, 28, 41, 44, 149, 157, 164, 183, 201
between   36, 45, 54, 114, 117, 123, 128, 134, 148, 174, 221,
239
beyond   218
biggest   38, 62, 156, 163
blinding   53
Blokdyk   9
boards 62
bodies 233
bottleneck   137
bought 11
bounce   52, 55
boundaries   25, 208
bounds   25
Breakdown   3-4, 64, 114, 129-130, 145
briefed 32

Briefly   148
brings   30
broken 50
brought   83
budget   64, 71, 97, 118, 131, 136, 149, 151, 159, 220, 226-
227, 229, 238
budgeting   132-133
budgets   94, 132, 167, 170, 220-221
building   22, 77, 222-223
burn-in 229
business   1, 8, 11, 19-21, 24-25, 29-30, 32, 36, 38-39, 49-51,
55, 59, 73, 77, 82-83, 87, 90, 93-94, 96-98, 103, 108, 118, 121-122,
163, 171, 179, 189, 191-193, 199, 220-221, 229, 233, 236
button 11
buy-in 83, 228
calculate   148
called 216
cancelled   233
candidates   232-233
cannot131-132, 143
capability   18, 45, 186, 203
capable   8, 30
capacities   90
capacity   18, 22, 113, 218
capital 87
capitalize   210
capture   39, 77, 127, 235
captured   44, 85, 118, 134-135, 154
career 123, 148, 170
careers   86
carried 183, 238
cascading   37
categories   175
category   24, 27
caused   1
causes 46, 48, 51-53, 71, 184, 220
causing   18, 220
celebrate   206
celebrated   211
certain 63, 173
certified   171, 233
chaired   9
challenge   8, 36

challenged   96
challenges   93, 171
Champagne   9
champion   25
champions   166
chance   184
change   5-6, 17, 27, 49-50, 61-62, 66, 76, 92, 101, 104, 110, 115, 119, 125, 129, 134, 138, 143, 160, 171, 178, 187, 191-193, 197-200, 214, 216, 221, 234-235
changed   27, 81, 94, 96, 122, 147, 157, 160, 175, 178, 186, 204
changes   19, 45, 58, 63, 66, 70, 77, 81, 86, 90, 115, 118, 127, 133, 146, 153, 159, 167-168, 197-199, 207, 213, 232, 235-236, 239
changing   83
channels   121, 191, 216
chargeable   131
charged   131
Charter   2, 28, 30, 108, 116, 154
charters   28
charting   135
charts 38, 43, 55
cheaper   41, 44
checked   75-77
checklist   9, 94
checklists   172
choice 24, 27, 83, 208
choices   147
choose   12, 66, 224
choosing   176
chosen106, 109, 193
circumvent   18
claimed   1
clarity 126
classes 172
classified   132, 188
cleaning   24
clearly 12, 17, 24, 27, 31, 34-35, 48, 57, 69, 80, 118, 121-122, 153, 169-171, 185-186, 189, 192, 209, 218
client   9, 11, 46, 92, 194, 229, 237
clients 27
closed 73, 153, 199, 234
closely 11, 151
Close-Out   7, 234-236

closest 88
Closing7, 50, 230
Closings   43
coaches   28, 31, 166
coalitions   112
coding 128
cognitive   212, 218
cognizant   211
colleague   89
colleagues   91, 150
collect 37, 74, 157, 166, 206
collected   28, 31, 40, 43, 54-55, 65
collection   38, 40-41, 43, 46, 52, 165, 238
college   58
combine   59
coming   50
command   74
comments   228, 238
commitment   93, 209
committed   26, 85, 176
Committee   162, 187, 189
common   108, 186
community   119, 158, 183
companies   1, 9, 148, 201
company   8, 41, 44, 50, 83, 89-90, 94-95, 98, 103-104, 148,
150, 171, 201, 220, 226
companys   226
compare   54, 61, 151, 222, 224, 238
compared   84, 159
Comparing   67
comparison   12
compatible   200, 218, 232
compelling   25
competitor   111, 221
complain   163
complaints   204
complete   1, 9, 12, 21, 26, 134, 136, 138-139, 142, 148-150,
163, 180, 209, 235
completed   13, 28-29, 32-33, 136, 143, 147, 175, 234
completely   97, 149
completing   89, 129, 143
completion   27, 30, 58, 118, 125, 142, 167, 206, 218, 223
complex   8, 44, 100, 127, 222

complexity   42, 197
compliance   50, 108, 128, 225
compliant   187
components   38, 43, 132
compute   13
computing   97
Concept   64, 165
concepts   127
concerns   19, 42, 88, 174, 214, 226
concrete   218
concurs   187
condition   73, 114
conditions   76, 81, 206, 232
conducted   63, 159, 161, 185-186, 239
conducting   50
confirm   13
Conflict   173
conflicts   152, 164
conjure   121
connecting   87
consensus   208
consider   18, 187
considered   19, 40, 202
considers   49
consistent   35, 75, 221
constant   220
Constraint   3, 127
consultant   8, 155
consulted   97, 174, 214
consulting   41
consults   52
consumers   94
contact   8, 117
contacts   102, 192
contain   18, 73
contained   1
contains   9
content   27, 201
contents   1-2, 9, 214
context   194
continual   11, 70, 73
continuity   36
contract   7, 117, 131-132, 142, 153, 187, 196, 225, 232-235

contractor   6, 120, 167-168, 188, 226
contracts   33, 131, 153, 193, 225-226, 234
control 2, 64, 69-70, 72-78, 119, 132, 134, 157, 193, 197-198, 202
controlled   49, 153, 175, 214, 220
controls   18, 50, 54, 64, 66, 72-73, 77-78, 142, 177, 184
convenient   42-43
convention   103
converge   218
convey   1
convince   171
cooperate   157
Copyright   1
corporate   203
correct 35, 69
corrected   233
corrective   71, 177
correctly   204
correspond   9, 11, 132
corruption   232
costing 36
counting   89, 136
counts 89
course 27, 222
covering   76
coworker   92
crashing   142
craziest   88
create 11, 19, 81, 83
created   50, 55, 96, 110, 115, 172, 176, 183, 190, 216
creating   8, 38
creativity   63
credible   157
crisis   23
criteria 2, 5, 9, 11, 24, 27, 29, 33, 66, 72, 84, 93, 102, 105, 121,
124-125, 157, 187-188, 191, 234
CRITERION   2, 17, 24, 35, 48, 57, 69, 80
critical 26-28, 43, 55, 70, 73, 85, 95, 114, 137, 154, 168, 188, 193,
202, 211, 230
criticism   50
criticized   211
crucial 55, 193-194
crystal 13
cultural 63

culture 29, 52, 169-170, 209
current 33, 35-36, 49, 51, 54, 71, 81, 88-89, 96, 102, 117, 122, 127, 135, 142, 165, 168, 170-171, 178, 191, 193, 197, 233
currently   25, 168, 220
custom 22
customer   11, 19, 25, 28-31, 45, 60, 69, 75, 86, 88-89, 96, 98-99, 122, 182, 195, 207
customers   1, 17, 29, 31, 33, 37, 39, 42-43, 45, 49, 54, 80, 83, 87-88, 91-92, 102, 176, 221, 225
cut-down   222
damage   1, 205
Dashboard   9
dashboards   70
databases   165
day-to-day   70, 87, 140
deadlines   19, 92, 140
dealer 171
deceitful   92
decide 65, 161, 169
decided   66, 206
deciding   80
decision   6, 49, 58-59, 62, 65-66, 170-171, 201, 208, 232
decisions   58, 66, 71, 78, 167, 169, 202, 206-207, 231
dedicated   8
deeper   13
deepest   9
deeply 179
defect 45, 172
defective   180
defects   39, 163, 198
define 2, 24, 26, 29-30, 42, 55, 108, 130, 149, 169, 202, 218
defined   12-13, 17-19, 24, 26-35, 39, 48-49, 57, 69, 80, 113, 125-126, 128-129, 131, 135, 153, 160, 163, 169-171, 186, 190, 209, 230, 239
defines 22, 25-26
Defining   8
definite   73
definition   127, 172, 176
degree   58, 210-213, 218-219
delays 136, 149
delegated   29
deletions   70
deliver 17, 26, 60, 85, 103, 157

delivered   44, 102, 190, 207
delivering   177
delivers   145
delivery   18, 81, 88, 140, 180, 191, 233-234, 236
Delphi 148
demand   102, 182, 233
demands   210, 218
department   8, 83, 117, 196, 220, 232-233
depend   195
dependent   88, 111
depends   94
depict 143
deploy 87, 203
deployed   70
deploying   41
derive 72
describe   21, 63, 109, 119, 123, 127, 198, 226-227, 238
described   1, 121, 125, 159, 199
describing   33
deserving   196
design 1, 9, 11, 24, 58, 63, 67, 74, 91, 103, 127, 168, 217
designed   8, 11, 50, 61, 63, 67
designing   8
desired26, 61, 146, 160, 223
detail   42-43, 65, 108-109, 130, 132, 134, 138, 150, 198
detailed   53, 55, 128, 132, 152
detect 76, 163
determine   11-12, 84, 88, 92, 136-137, 147, 157, 172
determined   53, 88, 117, 165, 181
determines   155
detracting   104
develop   57, 62, 68, 120, 129-130, 177
developed   9, 11, 28, 32, 47, 57, 66, 137, 159, 166, 171-172,
191, 199, 212, 222-223
developing   51, 65, 192
device 204, 212
devices   204, 209
diagnose   181
diagnostic   183
diagram   4, 53, 142-143
diagrams   127, 135
Dictionary   3, 131
differ   194

difference   114, 125, 134, 148, 202
different   8, 25, 31, 33, 53, 88, 111, 114, 135, 148, 170-171,
191, 201, 232
differs 187
difficult 145, 148, 155
difficulty   180
dilemma   92
direct 131, 221
direction   27, 41, 44
directions   183
directly 1, 49, 54
Directory   6, 206-207
Disagree   12, 17, 24, 35, 48, 57, 69, 80
disagrees   213
disaster   36
discarded   84
Disclosed   187
disclosure   132
discovered   66
discrete   198
discussed   201
discussion   45
display 43
displayed   28, 38, 40, 46, 52, 149
disposed   159
disputes   234
disqualify   85
disruptive   49
distribute   207
Divided   23, 29, 34, 47, 56, 68, 79, 104
division 116
document   11, 28, 128, 135, 202, 206, 238
documented 31, 47, 71, 75-77, 113, 126, 128, 135, 159, 170,
186, 197, 228, 230
documents   8, 133, 147, 151
domain   42
domains   89
dormant   102
double 233
drawing   181
driving 82, 100
duplicate   233
duration   4, 114, 129, 147-149, 183

durations   34, 134
during 27, 63, 106, 116, 128, 138, 144, 181, 183, 220, 233, 236, 238-239
dynamic   42
dynamics   33
earlier 81
earned   6, 147, 167, 222-223
economic   179, 183
economical   97
economy   59
eDiscovery   201-202
edition 9
editorial   1
education   20, 78, 204
effect 45, 117, 178, 180, 203, 239
effective   19, 89, 93, 99, 103, 128, 134, 183, 201, 203-204, 239
effects 41, 133, 140, 178, 206, 210
efficiency   49, 71
efficient   185, 195
effort   40, 45, 68, 97, 131, 214, 239
efforts 27, 109
electronic   1, 188
element   131-132
elements   11-12, 74, 88, 109, 131-132, 165, 168, 193-194, 198, 207, 220
Elevator   121
elicit   165
e-mail 121
embarking   25
embeddings 163
emergent   42
emerging   21, 75
employed   185
employee   65, 100, 212, 226
employees   54, 87, 91, 98, 104, 171, 212
employer   224
employers   110
empower   8
enable 49, 239
enablers   96
encourage   64, 75
end-users   176

engage   81, 174, 210, 219
Engagement   39, 110
engine 212
enhance   75, 78, 210
enhanced   86
enlarged   181
enough   8, 92, 94, 123, 189
ensure 28, 34, 66, 89-90, 93-95, 99, 108, 131, 165-166, 170-171, 190, 209, 225
ensures   94
ensuring   10, 94, 193, 222-223
entering   225
Enterprise   195
Entities 43
entity   1
entrance   203
equipment   18, 225
equipped   31
equitably   29
equivalent   154
errors   95
escalated   106
essence   108
essential   59
Essentials   101
establish   57, 157
estimate   40, 42-43, 149
estimated   27, 30, 40, 87, 153, 156-158, 226-227, 238
estimates   4, 30, 36, 54, 117, 127, 135, 147-148, 154-155, 159, 220
Estimating   4, 149, 154, 157
estimation   68, 147, 185
ethical 90, 203, 228
ethics   179
ethnic 83
evaluate   61, 64, 112, 181, 187
evaluated   204
evaluating   66, 233
evaluation   65, 74, 187-188, 210, 219
events 37, 61, 179
everyday   54
everyone   27, 30, 163
everything   202

evidence   13, 39, 164, 195
evolution   35
evolve 71
exactly 167, 203
example   2, 9, 14, 18, 55, 73, 132
examples   8-9, 11, 108, 113
exceed   129
exceeding   39
excellence   8
excellent   38
excessive   134, 180
exclude   58
execute   228
executed   40, 43, 199, 232
executing   5, 128, 153, 173, 193
execution   193, 206, 233
executive   8, 99, 189
executives   85
exempt   224
exerted   237
existence   179, 184
existing 11-12, 42-43, 73, 100, 109, 221
exists   142
expect 116, 150, 236
expected   19, 34, 99, 147, 193, 202
expecting   236
expend   40
expenses   221
expensive   44, 136, 149
experience   88-89, 91, 115, 150, 179, 204, 226, 236
experiment   104
Expert 9
expertise   59, 155
experts 34
expiration   142
explain 127
explained   11
explicit 203
explicitly   95
explore   53, 210, 219
exposure   177
extent 12, 32, 60, 113-114, 132, 212, 239
external   27, 82, 163, 180

extreme   210
facilitate   12, 18, 70, 218, 232
facility 232
facing 18, 92, 181
factor 120
factors 36, 45, 58, 95, 104, 108, 142, 158
failed   42
failing   100, 177
failure   40, 85, 128, 204, 230
fairly   29
familiar9
fashion 1, 33
feasible   43, 49, 104, 157, 175
feature10
features   229
feedback   2, 11, 29, 31, 42
figure   45
finalized   14
financial   38, 52-54, 85, 113, 203
financing   233
fingertips   10
finish   136, 139-140, 142, 222-223
finished   140
flying   24
focused   42
follow   11, 76, 93, 99, 228
followed   33, 128, 162, 172, 188, 238
following   9, 12
for--and   75
forecast   222
forefront   93
forever94
forget   10
formal 6, 100, 154, 161, 219, 228-229, 233, 238
formally   27, 132, 135, 152, 154
format 11
formats   175
formed26, 31
formula   13, 98
Formulate   24
formulated   208
forward   96, 100
foster   101-102

framework   74, 83, 165
freaky 92
frequency   33, 69
frequently   39, 44, 210, 219
friend   89, 92
frontiers   66
full-blown   39
full-scale   67
function   126, 153, 228, 232-233, 238
functional   131
functions   28, 51, 81, 86, 122, 126, 135, 169, 207, 232
funding   92, 96, 117, 127, 218
future   8, 43, 47, 76, 132, 171, 182
gained 52, 72, 75
gather 12, 35, 103
general   109, 139
generally   195
generate   50, 52, 68
generated   53, 65
generation   9
geographic   208
Gerardus   9
getting 128, 167, 174, 201, 214
glamor 24
global 59, 97, 141
governance   100, 135, 170, 213
governing   173
Government   131
graphs 9, 38
gratitude   9
grievance   204
ground 41, 53
grounded   232
groups 88, 117-118, 191, 196
growth 53, 103
guaranteed   24
guidance   1
guidelines   201
handle 144, 207, 209
handled   132, 209
handling   180-181
happen   17, 140, 177, 183, 192, 198, 203
happened   116, 198

happening   97, 183
happens   8, 11, 92, 94, 100, 157, 164, 184, 203, 213, 234
hardest   40
hardly 223
hardware   194
having 178, 204, 208
hazards   183
hazmat   224
health 175, 189
healthy   183
hearing   83
helpdesk   197
helpful 46
helping   8, 108
Herzberg   148
higher 132
high-level   29, 32, 121
high-tech   83
hijacking   87
hiring   58, 70
historical   157
history 136, 156
hitters 55
hitting 222
holders 107, 118
honest 90
humans   8
hypotheses   48
identified   1, 22, 25, 29-30, 38-41, 46, 50, 53-54, 113, 117,
121, 126, 131-132, 147, 153, 159, 164, 168, 172, 177, 185-186, 189,
201, 207, 214, 238
identify 12, 21-22, 42, 44, 50, 52, 54, 131-132, 157, 168, 173, 181,
187, 198
identity 210
ignoring   85
images 121
imbedded   75
immediate   41
impact 5, 26, 29, 36, 38-39, 41-43, 45, 58, 86, 106, 122, 159, 175,
177-179, 181-182, 187, 193, 199, 206, 213, 216, 230
impacted   191, 237
impacting   151
impacts   127, 150, 176, 236

Implement   22, 40, 69, 167
implicit 87, 203
importance   211
important   19, 36, 49, 54, 58, 86, 89, 91, 94, 99, 106, 109, 113,
120, 146, 163, 191, 194, 211, 230
improve   2, 11-12, 55, 57-61, 63-66, 107, 145, 163, 230-231,
238
improved   57, 59, 61, 64, 67, 74, 204
improving   61, 195
incentives   70, 212
include   58-59, 115, 147, 168, 187, 189
included   2, 9, 125, 127, 149, 157, 189, 197-198, 226-227,
234
includes   10, 41, 192
including   18, 27-28, 30, 38, 41, 49, 62, 64, 74, 77, 214, 220
increase   60, 90, 127
increased   170
increasing   86
incurring   131-132
in-depth   12
indicate   38, 73, 85, 102, 167
indicated   71
indicators   36, 46-47, 49, 54, 77, 131
indirect   131-132, 167, 221
indirectly   1
individual   1, 46, 136, 211, 219, 226, 232, 236
industry   84, 90, 96, 134
infected   183
infection   183
infinite 97
influence   66, 107, 110, 170, 173, 201, 214, 237
influences   141, 214
informal   218
informed   102, 118
ingrained   78
inhibit 63
initial   80, 151
initiated   158, 163, 199
Initiating   2, 90, 106
initiative   12, 166, 173
Innovate   57
innovation   49, 59, 74, 91, 101, 103, 141, 233
innovative   81, 114, 157

inputs 33, 50, 76, 107
inservice   233
insight 51
insights 9
inspired   88
Instead102
instructed   119
insure 96
insurers 62
integrate   74, 93
integrated   224
integrity   101, 199
intended   1, 62, 67, 178
INTENT 17, 24, 35, 48, 57, 69, 80, 203
intention   1
intentions   111, 203-204
interact   86
interest 173, 184, 196
interests   44, 174, 233
intergroup   210
interim 92
internal   1, 27, 82, 101, 140, 163, 189
interpret   12-13
intervals   189
interview   84, 236
interviews   232
introduce   42
introduced   24, 210
intuition   36
invalid 134
invaluable   2, 9, 11
inventory   156
investment   21, 161, 165, 179
investors   62
invoice206, 233
invoices   118
involve 102, 193
involved   17, 51, 65, 98, 111, 113, 120, 134, 153, 173, 176,
180, 186, 192, 196, 212, 235-236, 239
involves   72
involving   204
isolate 46

issues   66, 106, 112, 121, 126, 143-144, 151-153, 177, 185, 189, 203, 206-207, 214, 237-238

iteration   135

itself   1, 19, 135

joining 125

journey88

judgment   1

justified232

kicked 83

killer   81

knock-on   178

knowledge   11, 27, 44-45, 52, 59, 70, 72, 75, 78, 89, 95, 102-103, 234

labeling   204

lacked 96

languages   208

laptops   209

largely 51

latest   9

leader 19, 25, 52, 55, 209

leaders27, 31, 52, 82, 87, 214

leadership   30-31, 59, 87, 125, 209

learned   7, 71, 77, 85, 166, 185, 236-239

learning   74-75, 78, 201, 212

length 183

lesson 236-239

Lessons7, 67, 77, 85, 166, 185, 238-239

letter   121

levels   18, 33, 49, 54, 76, 96, 130, 134, 184

leverage   32, 59, 77, 88, 158, 191

leveraged   27

liability 1

licensed   1

lifeblood   88

lifecycle   39

lifecycles   59

Lifetime   10

likelihood   60, 67, 177, 183

likely   71, 89, 159, 179, 181-182

limited 11, 131

linked   32, 121, 201

listed   1, 165, 167, 185

listen   86, 208

location   208
logged171, 197
logical 143-144
longer 74
long-term   73, 87, 92
losses   47
lowest 132, 142, 220
machines   194
magnitude   60
maintain   69, 101, 103
maintained   219-220
majority   208
makers76, 171
making   19, 49, 58-59, 66, 82, 170, 208
manage   37, 55, 60, 92, 95, 108, 123-124, 138, 140, 155, 161, 165, 180, 214-215
manageable 30
managed   8, 32, 120, 171, 198, 233
Management 1, 3-5, 11-12, 19, 21, 23, 28, 30-31, 43-45, 52, 60, 62, 64, 66, 73, 88, 95, 99, 101, 106, 111, 113, 115-119, 125-128, 132, 134-135, 145, 148, 150, 153-154, 156, 160-161, 166-167, 169, 171, 173-176, 181, 185, 187, 189-192, 195, 203-204, 207, 216-217, 221, 223-225, 230, 233, 235
manager   8, 12, 22, 28, 30, 103, 119, 148, 172, 196, 228, 238
managers   2, 105, 148, 193-194
manages   109, 226
managing   2, 9, 105, 110, 203, 224, 237
mandatory   199
manner   128, 167, 185, 198, 205, 210, 228, 231
mantle97
mapped   29
market 43, 176, 221-222
marketable   176
marketer   8
marketing   91, 94, 121, 127, 140, 237
Maslow   148
master 151
material   140, 163, 188, 224
materials   1, 191
matrices   123
Matrix 3-5, 111, 123, 167, 181
matter 34, 36, 47, 210
maximize   179

maximizing   91
maximum   107
McClellan   148
McGregor   148
meaning   138, 208
meaningful   41, 87, 131-132
measurable   25, 29, 108, 156, 204, 212
measure   2, 12, 20, 22, 26, 32, 35-37, 39-40, 42, 44-46, 49-50, 57-59, 63-64, 70-71, 74-75, 78, 135, 157, 163-164, 181, 211, 220
measured   22, 35, 38-41, 43-45, 61, 76-77, 225
measures   37-40, 44-46, 49, 54, 73, 77, 114, 177, 183, 211-212, 232
measuring   131, 168
mechanical   1
mechanism   127, 236
mechanisms   165, 233
mechanized   134
medical   204
medium   210, 222
meeting   34, 36, 75, 166, 170, 195, 202, 207-209, 236
meetings   24, 26, 33, 119, 126, 171, 179, 189, 201, 233
megatrends   83
member   5-6, 31, 102, 167, 195, 208, 212-213, 215, 225
members   24, 28-30, 33, 120, 153, 173, 179, 186, 194, 207-211, 213, 218-219, 238
membership   218
method   24, 43, 98, 147, 149, 173, 191, 208, 211
methods   29, 33, 43, 157, 179, 185, 191, 204
metrics 4, 27, 45, 70, 119-120, 135, 154, 163, 191
milestone   4, 140, 147, 154
milestones   30, 110, 139, 153
minimal   210
minimize   175, 230
minimizing   91
minimum   34, 226
minutes   34, 65, 207, 233
missed 36, 83
missing 89, 167
mission 49, 53, 86, 91, 99, 109, 169
Mitigate   177, 230
mitigated   175
mitigating   117
mitigation   116, 147, 152, 189

mobile 209, 212
Modeling   51, 165
models 51, 84, 101, 111
modified   67, 198
module   120
moments   55
momentum   83, 89
monetary   21
monitor   62, 70-71, 74-75, 77-78, 157
monitored   71, 136, 147, 149
Monitoring   6, 70-71, 135, 144, 216
monthly   131
months 62, 65, 150
motivate   218
motivation   72, 76
motive 165
moving   96
multiple   185
myself 87
narrative   127
narrow 51
national   183
native 208
nature 42, 168
nearest   13
nearly 101
necessary   37, 50-51, 66, 76, 81, 86, 101, 131, 157, 160, 171,
179, 188, 204, 216
needed   18, 22, 33, 50, 65, 72-73, 77, 118, 149, 155, 171,
215, 225, 236
negatively   193, 237
negotiate   92
negotiated   101
neither 1
network   4, 142-143, 148, 218
Neutral 12, 17, 24, 35, 48, 57, 69, 80
nonlinear   163
normal 78, 147, 164, 183
Notice 1, 114, 147
notified   173, 192, 198, 235
notifies 164
notify   208

number   23, 34, 38, 47, 56, 68, 79, 82, 104, 138-139, 175, 180, 241
numerous   234-235
objective   8, 43, 168, 186, 201, 238
objectives   19-21, 24, 32, 49, 53, 72, 74, 85-86, 102-103, 113, 147, 161, 177-178, 186, 189, 195, 212, 233, 236
observed   62
obsolete   83
obstacles   18, 157
obtain 229, 236
obtained   31, 42
obvious   85
obviously   13
occurred   147, 178
occurring   60
occurs 23, 77, 182, 193
offerings   54, 61
offeror 187-188
Office 117, 154, 195, 235
officials 234
offshore   121
one-time   8
ongoing   43, 66, 76, 136, 149
on-going   117
online 11
on-site 206
operate   183, 208
operates   90
Operating   6, 75, 198, 208
operation   70
operations   12, 70, 74, 78, 204
operators   76, 163
opposite   90, 96
opposition   86
optimal   60, 64, 187, 226
optimally   203
Optimize   66, 78
optimized   82
option 83, 224
options 22
orders 232-233
organized   139, 233
organizm   183

orient   75
origin   122
original20, 151, 175, 201
originally   135, 171
Originate   76, 173
others 157, 159, 173-174, 176-177, 201, 218
otherwise   1, 63, 132, 159
outcome   13, 146, 206
outcomes   37, 46, 65, 68, 78, 102, 157, 178, 209, 217, 223
outlined   72
outlook   148
output 32, 37, 73, 76, 125
outputs   33, 50, 76, 144
outside64, 92, 171, 193
Outsource   108
overall 12-13, 20, 74, 103, 106, 127, 142, 161, 164, 192, 194, 202,
209, 227, 230
overcome   157
overhead   132, 167-168, 220-221
overheads   172
overlook   173
overlooked   107, 155, 185
overruns   132
oversight   117, 154, 189, 212
overtime   138
owners 129
ownership   34, 72
package   167
packages   132
packaging   204, 224
paragraph   98
parallel   142
parameters   70
Pareto 55, 135
particular   46, 55
Parties 115, 207, 234-235
partners   17, 87, 91, 94, 113, 236
pattern   139
paycheck   103
paying 94
payment   112, 118, 233-234
payments   117
payroll 224

pending 199
people 8, 22, 38, 50, 64-65, 71, 75, 78, 81-82, 86-88, 94, 100, 102, 128, 147, 163, 166-167, 171, 174, 179-181, 183, 186, 191, 196, 222
percent 81, 104
percentage 123
perception 57, 59, 90, 163
perform 22, 30, 32-33, 119, 128, 137, 148, 161, 184, 229
performed 66, 123, 136-137, 175-176, 187, 204, 206, 221
performing 187-188
perhaps 222
period 67, 168, 178, 212, 220
periodic 117
periods 198
permission 1
permit 42
person 1, 118, 173
personal 238
personally 123
personnel 21, 71, 143, 166, 189, 204, 233
pertinent 71
phases 39, 139
picked 98
planet 71, 78
planned 40, 43, 72, 77, 131-132, 137, 177-178, 209, 237
planners 76
planning 3, 9, 71, 73, 106, 108, 113, 128, 137, 143-144, 167, 195, 205
Planning- 77
platform 212
platforms 212-213
Pocket 149
Pockets 149
points 23, 34, 47, 55-56, 68, 78-79, 104, 140, 165
policies 96
policy 32, 76, 108, 135, 144, 178, 203, 224
political 63, 90, 173, 181, 214
population 114
portfolio 92, 194
portfolios 173
portray 55
position 170
positioned 157-158
positive 62, 83, 127, 210, 214

positively   237
possible   41-42, 51-52, 65, 68-69, 83, 97, 149, 172, 204
potential   19, 34, 42, 45, 60-61, 66, 83, 85, 100, 132, 168, 174, 183, 189, 216
practical   49, 57, 64, 69, 196
practice   37
practices   1, 11, 70, 77, 113, 229
praise   211
precaution   1
Predict 78
Prediction   178
prefer   184
preferred   191, 236
pre-filled   9
Premium   181
prepare   170
prepared   155
preparing   232
present   43, 76, 181, 194, 211
presented   198
preserve   33
pressures   140
prevent   47, 127-128, 135, 177, 205
prevented   233
preventive   183
prevents   19
previous   27, 140, 151, 164, 226
previously   118, 199
prices   220, 233
pricing 188
primary   120, 145, 220
printing   9
priorities   40, 46, 161
prioritize   182
priority 211
privacy   115, 225
probably   145, 181
problem   17-18, 20, 22, 24, 27, 29-30, 32, 49, 52, 112, 196, 198, 201, 221, 223
problems   18, 20-21, 46, 60, 62, 68, 71, 84, 122, 165, 216, 239
procedural   212
procedure   224

procedures   11, 75-77, 127, 144, 160-161, 165, 168, 188, 202, 225
proceed   179
process   1-8, 11, 25, 29, 32-33, 37-40, 43, 45-46, 48-55, 57-58, 62, 67, 69-70, 72-76, 78, 106, 108, 113, 116, 118-123, 125, 127-128, 135, 144, 149, 154, 165-166, 171, 175, 181, 188-189, 193-194, 202, 204, 206-208, 211, 216, 221-223, 226, 230-232, 237-238
processes   29, 36, 47, 49-51, 53, 55, 70, 73-74, 106, 113, 118, 128, 134, 165, 172, 175, 193, 198-199, 204, 229-230
produce   107, 144, 193, 196, 206
produced   62, 113, 126
producing   123, 125
product   1, 11, 40, 49, 54, 81, 99, 114, 117, 119, 125, 160, 175-176, 180-181, 194-196, 207, 214, 222-223, 228, 237, 239
production   66, 128
products   1, 18, 21, 38, 94, 108-109, 123, 132, 155, 160, 164, 171, 195, 216
profile 203, 205
Profitably   78
program   23, 58, 177, 216-217, 225, 233
programme   113
programs   62, 173, 196, 233
progress   32, 35, 64, 74, 82, 87, 113, 157, 204, 209, 211, 217
project 2-4, 6-9, 18, 21-22, 28, 39, 43, 51-52, 72, 81, 85, 87-88, 90, 96, 99-100, 102-103, 105-108, 110-111, 113-121, 123, 125-126, 128-130, 132, 134-136, 140, 142-143, 145-160, 168-172, 174-176, 178-182, 185-186, 189-190, 192-197, 199, 206-207, 214, 216-220, 222-226, 228-231, 234, 236-239
projects   2, 81, 84, 105, 113-114, 123, 130, 152, 161, 169, 173, 177, 179, 193-196, 206, 209, 222-224
promising   81
promote   38, 50
promotion   170
promptly   106
proofing   62
proper 131, 233
properly   11, 27-28, 45, 132-133, 197, 232
property   203
proposal   119, 140, 239
proposals   76, 187-188
proposed   22, 42, 63, 68, 115, 118, 120, 188-189, 226-227
protect   54, 97, 115
protection   91

protective   232
proved 229
provide   23, 51, 89-90, 98, 110, 114, 117, 122, 131, 142, 151, 154, 157, 210, 217, 219, 233
provided   9, 13, 70, 117, 153, 171, 187-188, 190, 239
providers   233
provides   121
providing   109-110
provision   135, 185, 201
publisher   1
pulled 81
purchase   9, 11, 232-233
purchased   11
purchases   189
purchasing   232
purpose   2, 11, 86, 145, 151, 157, 165, 197, 202, 210, 218-219
purposes   108, 132, 224
pursued   84
pushing   92
qualified   30, 153, 186
quality 1, 4, 6, 11, 37, 46, 48, 51-52, 75, 111, 117, 135, 148, 151, 153, 155, 161, 163-166, 169-170, 172, 185, 187, 197, 202-204, 216, 233
quantity   188
quarters   220
question   12-13, 17, 24, 35, 48, 57, 69, 80, 165, 208
questions   8-9, 12, 49, 238
quickly 12, 52, 55, 167, 175
radically   49
raised 185
rather 42, 102, 236
ratings 188
rationale   118, 171, 221
reaching   103
reactivate   102
Readiness   191
readings   77
realism 188
realistic   131, 134, 151, 194, 213
reality 203
realized   96, 229
really 8, 23

reason 80, 96
reasonable   102, 117, 189, 233
reasons   25, 118, 232
reassess   135, 185
rebuild 81
recasts 155
receive   9-10, 30, 37, 112, 191
received   32, 95, 179, 189, 239
recently   11, 99
recipient   234
recognize   2, 17-18, 21, 23, 60, 211
recognized   19-20, 58, 134, 210
recognizes   22
recommend   89, 92, 125
record 161
recorded   153, 161
recording   1, 208
records   21, 50, 131, 162, 220, 234
recovery   36, 128, 178
recruiting   148
Recurrence   183
redefine   24, 27
re-define   210
re-design   50
reduce 114, 134, 221
reducing   75, 86
references   241
reflect 52, 132-133
reform 39, 76, 104, 114
reforms 22, 42-43
regarding   97, 188, 195, 233, 239
Register   2, 5, 110, 173, 177
registered   233
regret 59
regular 26, 32, 171, 227
regularly   24, 28, 33, 171
regulated   198
regulatory   206
reject 119
rejected   197, 232
rejecting   119
relate 148, 199
related 37, 41, 72, 169, 173, 197, 223, 238

relation   22, 86, 111, 233
relations   71, 82
relative74, 211
relatively   100
release128, 135, 185
releases   226
relevant   11, 29, 43, 51, 74, 88, 170, 189, 206, 218, 233
reliable31, 184
Reluctance   213
remain 203, 220
remaining   157
remedial   47
remedies   41
Remember   149
remove   66
remunerate   65
repair 172
rephrased   11
replaced   113
replicated   236
Report 5-6, 37, 77, 187, 190, 195, 218, 226
reported   187, 222
reporting   72, 131-132, 175, 220
reports 37, 110, 126, 189, 198
repository   186
represent   61, 160
reproduced   1
reputation   85, 88
request   6, 49, 119, 160, 197, 199-200
requested   1, 58, 197, 199
requests   171, 197-198
require 39, 73, 144
required   18, 27, 32, 34, 62, 68, 107, 114, 118, 120, 136, 138,
147, 149, 165, 180-181, 194, 209, 217, 224-225, 233, 236
requires   188
requiring   110, 235
research   81, 111, 125, 148, 236
resemble   147
Reserve   155
reserved   1
reside 186
Resolution   51, 173
resolved   106, 151, 164, 185

Resource   4-5, 9, 117, 127, 138, 144-146, 148, 171, 176, 190, 195
resources   2, 9, 19, 26, 31, 45, 64, 68, 72-73, 82, 94, 96-97, 109, 111-112, 126, 134, 138-139, 143, 145, 153, 158, 160, 171, 190, 207, 215-216, 219, 225
respect   1
respond   113, 167, 208, 238
responded   13
response   23, 70-71, 73, 75, 227
responses   177-178, 187
responsive   158
result   50, 61-62, 114, 158, 160, 164, 199, 204, 218, 234, 236
resulted   73
resulting   53
results   9, 26, 34, 37, 54, 57-58, 60-61, 65, 67, 70, 77, 117, 139, 147, 158, 161, 164-165, 168, 193, 225, 229, 238
retain   80, 88, 162
retention   148
retrospect   81
return   44, 62, 142, 161, 165, 179
returned   24
revenue   41, 44
review 11-12, 109, 143, 185, 189, 202, 204, 233
reviewed   32, 107, 152, 189, 204, 232
reviewer   211
reviews 11, 117, 134, 161, 168
revised 54, 73, 184
revisions   235
reward 38, 46, 48, 196
rewarded   233
rewards   70
rights   1
roll-out 192
routine 74
safety   94, 115, 189
salvaged   204
Sampling   135, 161
satisfied   89, 156, 229, 237
satisfies 222
satisfying   81
savings 30, 54
scenario   194

schedule   3-4, 25, 43, 64, 71, 99, 114, 117, 120, 131, 134-135, 148, 151-152, 168, 176, 185, 200, 206, 216, 226, 230
scheduled   120, 171-172
Schedules   142
scheduling   132-134
scheme   73
Science   149
Scientific   149
Scorecard   2, 13-15, 193
scorecards   70
Scores 15
scoring 11
Screen 197
screening   164
seamless   96
second   13
seconds   208
section 13, 23, 34, 47, 55-56, 68, 78-79, 104
sections   128
sector 222
Secure 93
Securing   39, 95
security   20, 73, 110, 199, 225, 236
segmented   25
segments   31, 88, 221
select 48, 74
selected   64, 67, 115, 157, 182, 192
selecting   93
selection   5, 187, 211, 213, 232
sellers   1
selling 98, 140, 201, 220
senior 87, 99
sequence   137, 143
sequencing   104, 147, 172
series   12
seriously   111
servers 194
service 1-2, 8-9, 11, 40, 57, 59, 81, 84, 96, 178, 195-196, 233, 239
services   1, 9, 38, 41, 84, 89, 187, 194, 203, 221, 226, 228, 234
serving 204
session 137
setbacks   52, 55

several 9
severely   50
Severity   178
shared 72, 158, 201, 209
sharing 75, 191, 221
sheets 119
shorten 151
short-term   179
should 8, 19, 25, 29, 37, 40-41, 48, 50, 57-58, 61, 64, 67, 71-72, 74,
82-83, 86-87, 100-101, 110-111, 114, 116, 120, 125, 132, 136, 145,
149, 152-153, 155, 159, 170, 175, 177-178, 180-182, 187, 192, 194,
197-198, 212, 216, 230, 239
-should 159
signature   95
signatures   144
signed 225
signers 234
silent   209
similar 27-28, 54-55, 61, 118, 136, 139, 156, 163, 179
simple 100, 212, 222
simply 9, 11
single   98, 209
single-use   8
situation   18, 35, 181, 186, 193, 221-222
situations   210
skeptical   94
skills   18, 37, 42-43, 89, 102-103, 155, 172, 179, 210, 213, 219,
238
smallest   20, 62
social   91, 94, 183, 210, 224, 232
software   18, 119-120, 135, 154, 190, 194, 224-226
solicit 29
soluiton   226
solution   44, 49, 51, 57-58, 60, 63-64, 66-67, 69, 227
solutions   39, 42-43, 61, 63, 65-68
someone   8, 232
someones   211
something   101, 116, 160
Sometimes   39
Source 5, 96, 184, 187
sources   53, 55, 66, 103, 181
special 9, 70, 188

specific   9, 19, 21, 25, 29, 32, 93, 128, 140, 144-145, 148, 155, 170, 186, 191, 196, 199, 211
specified   103, 131-132, 220
Speech   121
spoken 99
Sponsor   19, 115, 118, 126, 134, 171
sponsored   25
sponsors   17, 171
stability 45
stable 176, 224
staffed 26
staffing 18, 70, 127, 203
staffs   212
stages 135, 185, 232
standard   8, 144, 226-227
standards   1, 11-12, 78, 90, 163, 166, 199, 203
started 9, 140, 143
starting 12
startup 93
stated 93, 95, 122
statement   3, 12, 62, 68, 91, 125-126, 132, 160
statements   13, 23, 29-30, 34, 47, 52, 56, 68, 79, 104, 147, 165, 203
status 5-6, 50, 111, 131-132, 178, 189, 195, 197, 220, 222-223, 226
statutory   206
Steering   162, 189
stopper   122
storage   165
stored 205
strategic   71, 74, 86, 161, 177, 186, 189, 203
-Strategic   73
strategies   86, 113, 148, 152, 189, 201
strategy   20, 65-66, 77, 82, 91, 103, 176, 178, 192, 202, 221, 236
strengths   229
striving 108
stronger   104
Strongly   12, 17, 24, 35, 48, 57, 69, 80, 197
structure   3-4, 64, 100, 114, 129-130, 145, 181, 187, 191
structures   167
stubborn   92
stupid 82

subdivided   132
subject9-10, 34
Submit 11, 197
submitted   11, 199
subsequent   134
subset 20
subtotals   155
succeed   94
success   22, 26, 36, 39-40, 42, 45, 60, 77, 81, 85, 87-88, 95, 98, 102, 104, 106, 142, 156, 171, 190-191, 194-195, 202, 230
successful   53, 66, 70, 85, 88, 103, 113, 147, 193, 196
successor   135
sufficient   43, 113-114, 181, 204, 213, 239
suggest   205
suggested   71, 160
suitable   38
summarize   148
summarized   132
Supervisor   208, 212
supplier   86, 171
suppliers   33, 49, 87, 233
supplies   171, 229
Supply 84
support   8, 49, 66, 70, 78, 86, 89, 99, 117, 122, 134, 144, 161, 169, 178, 201, 227, 239
supported   26, 48, 175
Supporting   62
supportive   170
surface   71
Surveys9
SUSTAIN   2, 66, 80
sustaining   73, 140, 208
symptom   17
system 11-12, 49, 74, 87-88, 109, 119, 121-122, 125, 127, 131, 145, 168-169, 176, 199, 201, 203-204, 222-223
systematic   40, 42
systems   41-42, 48-49, 60, 70, 81, 118, 161, 189, 212, 223
tables 127
tackled   96, 112
tactics 201
takers 126
taking 41, 44, 114, 195
talents 102

talking 8
tallied 159
target 31, 114, 154, 191
targeted   212
targets 111, 156, 222
tasked 72
Teaches   52
teaming   209
technical   59, 63, 187-188
technique   43, 148
techniques   51-52, 101, 107, 180
technology   81, 96, 113, 148, 175, 180, 182, 204, 208-209
template   151
templates   8
tenders   232
Test-Cycle   165
tested 21, 65, 233
testing 64, 66, 128
Thamhain   148
thankful   9
themselves   42, 100, 104
theories   148
theory 72, 76
therefore   183
things 61, 93, 106-107, 125, 155, 163, 217, 230
Thinking   52, 64, 91, 103
thorough   159
thought   214
threat 95
threaten   111
threatened   111
threats 128, 184
through   51, 87, 132
throughout   1, 127, 220
tighter 94
time-based   168
time-bound   29
timeframe   157
timeline   200
timely 33, 167, 185, 198, 206, 231
Timescales   140
timetable   142
Timing 206

together   81, 212
tolerable   184
tolerance   120
tolerated   150
tomorrow   71, 78, 103
top-down   74
topics 59
touched   121
toward 75, 195
towards   51, 114
tracking   25, 74, 127-128, 134, 154
traction   94
trademark   1
trademarks   1
tradeoff   188
trade-offs   117
trained 26-27, 29, 179, 190
training   22, 64, 70, 77-78, 115, 128, 179, 192, 195, 204,
212-213, 233, 239
Transfer   13, 23, 34, 47, 56, 68, 70, 72, 79, 104, 226
transition   119
translated   25
transport   224
trends 21, 49, 54, 163, 179, 183
Tricky 84
triggers 118
trophy 97
trouble 81
trying 8, 50, 87, 90, 108, 163
typical 107, 214
ubiquitous   97
ultimate   100
underlying   60
undermine   90
underruns   132
understand   28, 170, 181, 194, 208, 213, 219
understood   81, 95, 168, 218, 225
undertake   53
underway   58
uninformed   102
unique 140, 160
uniquely   214
unknown   184

Unless 8
unpriced   220
unresolved   135, 144
update   160, 237
updated   9-10, 52, 117, 131, 135, 142, 190, 197
updates   10, 70, 227
updating   154
urgent 197
usability   92
useful 63, 75, 130, 155, 176
usefully 12, 20
utility   150
utilized 212
utilizing 58
validate   223
validated   29, 32, 53, 107
Validation   223
Validity 122
valuable   8
values 87, 183
variables   37, 48, 76, 202
variance   6, 211, 220
variances   168, 221
variation   17, 34, 38, 40, 43, 46, 53, 55, 75
variety 64
various 111, 135, 185
vendor 118, 142, 232
vendors   21, 93
verbiage   216
verified 10, 29, 32, 53, 107
verify   71, 74, 76, 125, 222, 234
version 226, 241
versions   25, 33
versus 209
vested 184
vetting 127
viable 129
vice-versa   236
vigorously   218
violations   127
Virgin   24
vision   87, 91, 169
visualize   149

voices 110
volatile 59
volume   220
warrant   206
warranty   1, 198
weaknesses   111, 128, 229
wealth 42-43
website   197
weighted   148
whether   8, 72, 80
-which 173
wholesaler   171
Wilemon   148
willing 159, 224
windfall   115
winning   233
win-win   221
within   53, 67, 131, 136, 138, 149, 169, 183, 185, 189, 195, 199,
207-208, 229
without1, 13, 44, 81, 103, 122, 131, 151, 179, 200, 235
worked   58, 106, 156, 185
workers   83
Workflow   1-7, 9-15, 17-23, 25-34, 36-63, 65-69, 71-108, 110-
111, 113-121, 123, 125-132, 134-136, 138, 140, 142-161, 163, 165,
167-183, 185-187, 189-197, 199, 201, 203, 206-210, 212, 214, 216-
220, 222-226, 228-232, 234, 236-240
-Workflow   71
workforce   18, 81, 87-88
working   62, 72, 111, 128, 169, 177, 182, 202
Worksheet   4, 149, 157
writing 11, 123, 161
written 1, 203, 225
year-end   131
yourself   50, 102, 170, 194